Global Sociology and the Struggles for a Better World

SAGE STUDIES IN
INTERNATIONAL SOCIOLOGY

Series Editor Chaime Marcuello Servós (2016–ongoing)
Professor, Department of Psychology and Sociology,
Zaragoza University, Spain

This monograph presents revised contributions of the Opening and Closing Plenaries of the Third ISA Forum of Sociology in Vienna, Austria, July 2016. The Forum was organized by ISA Vice-President Markus S. Schulz on the theme 'The Futures We Want: Global Sociology and the Struggles for a Better World'. The authors are renowned sociologists from different continents who explore challenges and opportunities of our era with complementary theoretical lenses and deep regional expertise. See also the accompanying WebForum: http://futureswewant.net.

Global Sociology and the Struggles for a Better World

Towards the Futures We Want

Edited by **Markus S. Schulz**

SSIS SERIES SAGE STUDIES IN INTERNATIONAL SOCIOLOGY: 66

Los Angeles | London | New Delhi
Singapore | Washington DC | Melbourne

Los Angeles | London | New Delhi
Singapore | Washington DC | Melbourne

SAGE Publications Ltd
1 Oliver's Yard
55 City Road
London EC1Y 1SP

SAGE Publications Inc.
2455 Teller Road
Thousand Oaks, California 91320

SAGE Publications India Pvt Ltd
B 1/I 1 Mohan Cooperative Industrial Area
Mathura Road
New Delhi 110 044

SAGE Publications Asia-Pacific Pte Ltd
3 Church Street
#10-04 Samsung Hub
Singapore 049483

Editor: Natalie Aguilera
Editorial assistant: Eve Williams
Production editor: Katherine Haw
Copyeditor: Elaine Leek
Proofreader: Bryan Campbell
Indexer: Elizabeth Ball
Marketing manager: George Kimble
Cover design: Wendy Scott
Typeset by: C&M Digitals (P) Ltd, Chennai, India
Printed in the UK

Editorial arrangement © Markus S. Schulz 2019

Chapter 1 © Markus S. Schulz 2019
Chapter 2 © Jan Nederveen Pieterse 2019
Chapter 3 © Todd Gitlin 2019
Chapter 4 © Stephan Lessenich 2019
Chapter 5 © Akosua Adomako Ampofo 2019
Chapter 6 © Nora Garita Bonilla 2019
Chapter 7 © Asef Bayat 2019
Chapter 8 © Saskia Sassen 2019
Chapter 9 © Michel Wieviorka 2019
Chapter 10 © Alain Touraine 2019

First published 2019

Library of Congress Control Number: 2018939216

British Library Cataloguing in Publication data

A catalogue record for this book is available from the British Library

ISBN 978-1-5264-6399-9
ISBN 978-1-5264-6398-2 (pbk)

At SAGE we take sustainability seriously. Most of our products are printed in the UK using responsibly sourced papers and boards. When we print overseas we ensure sustainable papers are used as measured by the PREPS grading system. We undertake an annual audit to monitor our sustainability.

Contents

About the Editor and Contributors

Markus S. Schulz is Vice-President for Research of the International Sociological Association (2014–18) and President of the Third ISA Forum of Sociology. Passionate about teaching, he taught a wide range of courses across social science disciplines at the Bauhaus University of Weimar, University of Illinois at Urbana-Champaign, Virginia Tech, New York University, and the New School for Social Research, where he also completed his PhD. Schulz is Research Associate of the Fondation Maison de Science Social and Fellow at the Max Weber Centre for Advanced Cultural and Social Studies. He won for his research international recognition, including the Bielefeld Prize for the Internationalization of Sociology, the Candace Rogers Award, and Elise Boulding Award. Schulz edited for the ISA journal *Current Sociology* special issues on *Future Moves* and on *Values and Culture*. He co-authored the six-volume book series on *Internet and Politics in Latin America* (Vervuert, Germany). Among his articles in English are 'Collective action across Borders: Opportunity structure, network capacity and communicative praxis in the age of advanced globalization' (*Sociological Perspectives* 41:3) and 'Debating futures: Global trends, alternative visions, and public discourse' (*International Sociology* 31:1). Schulz is founding curator of the WebForum, http://futureswewant.net. Author website http://markus-s-schulz.net.

Contributors

Akosua Adomako Ampofo is Professor of African and Gender Studies at the University of Ghana, Legon, where she has been a Research Fellow at the Institute of African Studies since 1989, and until July 2015 was its Director. She is a founding member and current president of the African Studies Association of Africa. Adomako Ampofo considers herself an activist scholar and was also the founding Director of the Centre for Gender Studies and Advocacy, CEGENSA, at the University of Ghana (2005–2009). Her teaching, research and advocacy address issues of African knowledge systems; higher education; identity politics; gender-based violence, women's work, masculinities and gender representations in popular culture (music and religion). Adomako Ampofo is Co-editor, with Cheryl R. Rodriguez and Dzodzi Tsikata, of *Transatlantic Feminisms: Women's and Gender Studies in Africa and the Diaspora* (Lexington Books, 2015), and with Kwasi Ampene, Albert Awedoba and Godwin K. Adjei, of *A Festschrift in Honour of Emeritus Professor J. H. Kwabena Nketia* (University of Michigan Press, 2015). She is a member of CODESRIA, the (US) African Studies Association, and immediate past Co-President of the Research Committee on Women and Society of the International Sociological Association. She is Co-editor, *Critical Investigations into Humanitarianism in Africa* blog, www.cihablog.com, and editor, *African Studies Review*; and editor-in-chief of *Contemporary Journal of African Studies.* She tweets at @adomakoampofo.

Asef Bayat is the Catherine and Bruce Bastian Professor of Global and Transnational Studies and Professor of Sociology and Middle Eastern Studies at the University of Illinois at Urbana–Champaign. Bayat had previously taught for many years at the American University in Cairo and served as the director of the International Institute for the Study of Islam in the Modern World (ISIM) at Leiden University in the Netherlands, while also holding visiting positions at the University of California at Berkeley, Columbia University, Oxford, and Brown. He has been awarded fellowships from the Ford, Guggenheim, MacArthur, and Open Society Foundations. Among his most recent books are *Post-Islamism: The Changing Faces of Political Islam* (Oxford University Press, 2013); *Life as Politics: How Ordinary People Change the Middle East* (Stanford University Press, 2nd edn, 2013) and *Revolution without Revolutionaries: Making Sense of the Arab Spring* (Stanford University Press, 2017).

Nora Garita Bonilla is President of the Latin American Sociological Association (Asociación Latinoamericana de Sociología, ALAS). She obtained her doctorate at the University of Paris X Nanterre, France, and is Professor of Sociology at the University of Costa Rica, where she also directs the Center for Investigation and Studies of Women (Centro de investigación y estudios de la mujer, CIEM). She has organized the XXX Congress of ALAS in Costa Rica 2015 on the theme 'Pueblos en movimiento' ('Communities in Movement').

Todd Gitlin is Professor of Journalism and Sociology and Chair of the PhD program in communications at Columbia University, and the author of 17 books, including *The Whole World Is Watching* (UC Press, 1980/2003), *The Sixties: Years of Hope, Days of Rage* (Bantam, 1987), *The Twilight of Common Dreams: Why America Is Wracked by Culture Wars* (Metropolitan, 1995), *Media Unlimited: How the Torrent of Images and Sounds Overwhelms Our Lives* (Metropolitan, 2003) *Occupy Nation: The Roots, the Spirit, and the Promise of Occupy Wall Street* (HarperCollins, 2012), and a just-completed novel, *The Opposition* (HarperCollins, 2012). Author website: http://toddgitlin.net/.

Stephan Lessenich is Professor in the Department of Sociology, Ludwig Maximilians University, Munich (Germany). Professor Lessenich's research interests are: political sociology, social policy and the welfare state, modern capitalism and capitalist dynamics. Recent publications have been: *Claus Offe and the Critical Theory of the Capitalist State* (with Jens Borchert, Routledge, 2016); *Capitalism, Sociology, Critique* (with Klaus Dörre and Hartmut Rosa, Verso, 2015) and *Living Well at Others' Expense: The Hidden Costs of Western Prosperity* (Polity, 2019).

Jan Nederveen Pieterse is Duncan and Suzanne Mellichamp Distinguished Professor of Global Studies and Sociology at University of California Santa Barbara. He specializes in globalization, development studies and cultural studies, and focuses on 21st-century trends. He held the Pok Rafeah Distinguished Chair at Malaysia National University, 2014–2015. Recent books are *Multipolar Globalization* (Routledge, 2018), *Globalization and Culture: Global Mélange* (Rowman & Littlefield, 4th edn, 2019), *Development Theory: Deconstructions/Reconstructions* (Sage, 2010), *Is There Hope for Uncle Sam?* (Zed Books, 2008), *Ethnicities and Global Multiculture* (Rowman & Littlefield, 2007). He edits book series with Routledge (Emerging Societies) and Palgrave MacMillan (Frontiers of Globalization).

Saskia Sassen is the Robert S. Lynd Professor of Sociology and former Chair, Committee on Global Thought, Columbia University. Her books include *Expulsions: Brutality and Complexity in the Global Economy* (Harvard University Press, 2014, translated into 12 languages); *Cities in a World Economy*, 5th fully updated edition (Sage, 2018); *Losing Control: Sovereignty in an Age of Globalization*, The Schoff Memorial Lectures (Columbia University Press, 1995, New updated edition 2016); *Territory, Authority, Rights: From Medieval to Global Assemblages* (Princeton University Press, 2008); *A Sociology of Globalization* (W.W. Norton, 2007); *The Global City* (Princeton University Press, 1991) and *The Mobility of Labor and Capital* (Cambridge University Press, 1988). Her books have been translated into over 20 languages. She is the recipient of diverse awards and mentions, multiple doctor *honoris causa*, named lectures and selected for various honors lists. She was awarded the Principe de Asturias 2013 Prize in the Social Sciences, and selected as one of the top 100 women in the Sciences in 2018. Author website: www. saskiasassen.com.

Alain Touraine is Professor at the École des Hautes Études en Sciences Sociales in Paris, France, where he founded the Centre d'analyse et d'intervention sociologiques (Center for Sociological Analysis and Intervention, CADIS). He has been awarded distinguished prizes for his lifetime work, by the ISA as well as by other organizations and countries, including the Príncipe de Asturias Prize and inclusion in the French Légion d'Honneur. Among his most influential books are: *The Post-Industrial Society* (1971), *The Self-Production of Society* (1977), *The Voice and the Eye* (1981), *Critique of Modernity* (1995), and *Thinking Differently* (2009).

Michel Wieviorka is Professor at the École des Hautes Études en Sciences Sociales and President of the Fondation Maison des Sciences de l'Homme, both in Paris. He has been President of the ISA (2006–2010).

1

Introduction: Global Sociology and the Struggles for a Better World

Markus S. Schulz

The contemporary world has reached a pivotal moment of escalating injustices and apocalyptic risks, but also of unprecedented opportunities. Mounting pressures of social and ecological problems are met by a confluence of intellectual trends that allow the questioning of entrenched assumptions and the unleashing of a forward-oriented sociological imagination. This monograph explores pertinent trends, alternative visions, and new directions for sociological research. The Introduction provides in its first part a brief sketch of the social, historical, and intellectual context of sociology's forward-turn and in its second part an overview of key arguments developed in the individual chapters. The diversity of theoretical approaches and regional expertise reflect the complexity of challenges and the multiplicity of future projects on a shared planet.

Opening Futures

Not long ago, during the 1990s, the Washington Consensus of neoliberal policies emerged so victorious from the Cold War that the 'end of history' appeared as its mantra. In contrast, the current *Zeitgeist*, or 'spirit of the time', appears better captured by the notion of 'crisis'. Yet, there is something inherently puzzling about this new crisis discourse (Schulz 2016c). A financial crisis has shaken much of the world, but instead of giving way to a new economic regime, the previously established neoliberal templates persist like zombies. Billions of dollars were mobilized almost overnight to rescue banks, but austerity was imposed on the many. Today, broad sectors of European populations worry about a 'refugee crisis', while the refugees themselves worry about even more fundamental crises. For human livelihood on the planet, the specter of climate change has become ever harder to ignore and gives 'crisis' yet another dimension of meaning. The many 'morbid symptoms' of our time seem to fit Antonio Gramsci's famous characterization of 'crisis' as an 'interregnum' in which 'the old is dying and the new cannot be born'. This raises the questions: What could then lead to the new? What role could sociology play in the inventing of the new?

The widespread lack of future imagination has been noted over the past few decades in a number of time-diagnoses by authors as diverse as Alvin Toffler, Norbert Elias, Jürgen Habermas, Claudio Lomnitz, and Slavoj Žižek. For example, the futurist Toffler argued in his famous *Future Shock* (1970) that 'Change is avalanching upon our heads and most people are grotesquely unprepared to cope with it.' Historical sociologist Elias (1987) came to similar conclusions within a yet longer time-frame when he wrote: 'Today we have basically lost the ability to think of a future. Most people do not want to go beyond their present – they do not like to see themselves as a link in the chain of generations.' Discussing political implications, critical theorist Habermas (1985) spoke of an 'exhaustion of utopian energies' that hampered the 'legiti- macy crisis' of Western welfare-states. The anthropologist Lomnitz (2003) diagnosed in the Mexican context a 'present saturation' that 'dis- ables constructive futures engagements'. The philosopher Žižek (2011) argued that the Western imagination is so curtailed that it needs no cen- sorship, as its movies can show apocalyptic asteroid collisions but are unable to depict a future beyond capitalism.

Yet, futures thinking does take place; it is just not well distributed. Naomi Klein (2001) has prominently shown how elites use 'shock' during 'crises' to impose blueprints faster than civil societies can mount resist- ance. Now a question for sociology: How could this be turned around? What could make publics from the grassroots stronger, unleash their imaginative capacities, and lend them more efficacy? What does it take to democratize futures?

Before tackling this question, it is worthwhile to reflect on how aca- demia and the social sciences relate to anticipative thinking. How do disciplines differ in taking a position *vis-à-vis* the future? For one, the prominent anthropologist Arjun Appadurai (2013) has recently castigated his discipline for neglecting the future. Appadurai criticized that 'anthro- pology remains preoccupied with the logic of reproduction, the force of custom, the dynamics of memory, the persistence of habitus, the glacial movement of the everyday, and the cunning of tradition in the social life of even the most modern movements and communities'.

Yet, would a similar verdict not apply to sociology too? Have sociologists neglected the future perhaps even more spectacularly or at least failed to address it in terms that are more explicit? In business schools, it is quite common to see course offerings on the future. Marketing research revolves around studies about the anticipation of consumer choices and trends. Some of the brightest students are being taught how to devise algorithms for fast-paced trading in financial derivatives, so that profits can be made from 'futures', before anyone else even thinks about them. Yet, future courses are largely absent from the sociology curricula in most countries.

Such avoidance of the 'future' was not always the case. To the contrary, the classic founding figures of sociology were driven by their interest in the future. As religious beliefs in some future telos gave way to the positivist search for social laws during the discipline's formative period in Western Europe, sociologists in traditions from Auguste Comte to Emile Durkheim thought this kind of knowledge to be useful for managing or administrating society. At the opposite end of the spectrum, Karl Marx shared underlying assumptions when he pronounced the laws of history would be pointing to a necessary triumph of the oppressed, though he did recognize in his more empirical writings that there were no historical automatisms but plenty of maneuvering room for contingent action. Throughout his life, W.E.B. DuBois sought synergies between sociology and open political activism. Pioneering feminist sociologist Charlotte Perkins Gilman came to broad fame as author of a best-selling utopian novel, *Herland* (1979 [1915]), the story of an alternative world governed by women.

The belief in an open future has been understood as the hallmark of the modern consciousness of time. As the historian Reinhart Koselleck (2004 [1979]) noted, the 'space of experience' and the 'horizon of expectation' are increasingly disassociated. This fundamental contingency opens the horizon of the possible for social and political creation. What is could have been different. The existing reality could have been differently shaped through non-determined human action, in more or less reflexive as well as in more or less conflictive or cooperative ways.

The striking absence of explicit 'future' engagements in the contemporary sociology of many countries can be seen as a by-product of a defensive strategy aimed at gaining respectability by emulating the supposedly rigorous methods of the 'hard sciences' while avoiding the inherently unpredictable. However, the time seems now ripe to re-examine such premises in a broader way. There are at least four crucial intellectual trends that prepare the ground and shape such rethinking.

First, scholars from or engaged with the Global South have challenged static, determinist orthodoxies and emphasized the conflictive nature of knowledge. I refer here to the work of scholars as diverse as Fernando Henrique Cardoso and Enzo Faletto (1969), Andre Gunder Frank (1978), Samir Amin (1976), Anibal Quijano (2000), Edward Saïd (1978), Dipesh Chakrabarty (2000), Gayatri Spivak (1985), Jan Nederveen Pieterse (2000), Sujata Patel (2010), Orlando Fals Borda (1978), Silvia Rivera Cusicanqui (1987), Paulo Henrique Martins (2012), Arturo Escobar (2009), Alberto Bialakowsky (2013), Maristella Svampa (2005), and José Vicente Tavares dos Santos (2015), among others. Sociology at large benefits from debates and collaboration across borders. Although the Global South is severely underrepresented in global discourse, its intellectual impact is felt. This impact is not confined to studies of areas in the Global South, but, as especially Chakrabarty (2000) and Quijano (2000) emphasized, they also helped scholars in the North to recognize its relational constitution *vis-à-vis* the South and to learn viewing it not as a kind of universal yardstick but as one province among others within a complex world.

Second, there is increased attention to contingency, choice, and creativity across vastly different theory types and research approaches from the micro to the macro. This new sensibility is expressed in the increased use of concepts such as 'creativity of action,' (Joas, 1997), 'expectation, choice, and decision,' (Bell, 1997a, 1997b), 'human agency,' (Emirbayer and Mische, 1998), 'reflexivity,' (Beck, 1992; Beck et al., 1994), 'imagination' (Bello, 2001; Boulding and Boulding, 1995; Castoriadis, 1975; Masini, 1993; Sassen, 2007; Sztompka, 1993), the 'multiplicity' of historical trajectories (Eisenstadt, 2003; Featherstone et al., 1996; Nederveen Pieterse, 2000, 2007), 'uncertainty' (Wallerstein et al., 2013), 'utopistics' (Wallerstein, 1998), and postcolonial alternatives (Bonfil Batalla, 1987; Coronil, 1996; Dussel, 1995; García Canclini, 1989; Lander, 1997; Patel, 2010; Quijano, 2000). Even systems theory recognized the need to ascribe to 'systems' an 'autopoietic' capacity for generating futures (Herrera Vega, 2010; Luhmann, 1995). Yet let me emphasize: Agency is not just about what we do not want, i.e. not merely about resistance against something, but it is also – and crucially – about creating entirely novel ideas and new visions (Schulz, 2009).

Third, Michael Burawoy's (e.g. 2004, 2008; Schulz, 2016a) passionate advocacy of what he prominently called 'public sociology' helped sociologists to reach out to and engage with publics, especially in countries, such as the United States, where sociologists used to be largely confined to the Ivory Tower. For example, sociological trend projections or forecasts can serve publics as warnings about what might happen if no countermeasures are being taken (Schulz, 1999). Scenario building adds to these specific visions and extrapolations of alternative paths (Schulz, 2001). Studies of the imaginary bring in notions of power and can relate to subaltern social actors with counter-hegemonic projects (Schulz, 1998). And research on values can help to spell out the value choices that are often only implicit in alternative futures (Bachika and Schulz, 2011; Schulz, 2011, 2015). Erik Olin Wright's recent work on 'real utopias' (2010) locates the prefigurations of broader alternative futures in present practices, projects, and institutions, thereby demonstrating their principle viability.

Fourth, social movements and contentious practices in everyday life keep critical thought about alternative futures alive (cf. Bayat, 2010; Bloch, 1959; Mannheim, 1936; Schulz, 2016b; Touraine, 1981; Touraine et al., 1983). The 'Washington Consensus' and the 'end of history' were not without dissenters. The hegemony of the neoliberal agenda met its resistance. To provide some examples, austerity measures along with the de-socialization of water and other natural resources provoked massive protests in South American countries such as Argentina, Bolivia, Ecuador, and Venezuela. Popular unrest gave way to the 'pink tide', the election of a new brand of populist governments in many countries of the region. In Mexico, on the first day of January 1994 when NAFTA, the North American Free Trade Agreement took effect, some 3,000 indigenous peasants rose up in arms against the government's authoritarian imposition of a neoliberal development project that threatened to convert rural subsistence farmers into a slum-dwelling urban proletariat (Schulz, 1998). The Zapatista critique of neoliberalism became a central reference point of the alter-globalization movement (Schulz, 2014). Over the years, the Zapatistas managed to surprise time and again with creative activities that connected local struggles with national and even transnational movements. They built communities of resistance with a whole new generation of activists struggling for alternative futures with dignity. The Zapatistas' resistance is simultaneously political, economic, social, and cultural. It is about making self-governance and subsistence work, creating a social model with inherent appeal. Their answer to the question of social justice starts with freedom. They do not ask for permission, but they do things. Structural adjustment policies have increased urban slums worldwide; it is time to recognize development innovation from the ground up. A sociology with global aspirations and attuned to the problems of inequality can benefit from close listening to the voices at the grassroots.

Approaching Futures

This monograph presents contributions by distinguished sociologists from different continents about 'The Futures We Want: Global Sociology and the Struggles for a Better World'. The chapters are revised and elaborated papers that the authors presented at the Opening and Closing Plenaries of the International Sociological Association's Third Forum of Sociology, held on this theme in Vienna, Austria, in July 2016.[1] The presenters were selected for their insights on the crucial issues of our time and in an effort to include contrasting theoretical approaches and complementary regional expertise. The following section provides an overview of their contributions to this volume.

Jan Nederveen Pieterse takes a bird's-eye perspective on major global and transnational trends, distinguishing how these are positive, negative, or ambiguous in their effect on social inequalities. In balance, Nederveen Pieterse sees a long-term structural shift with the rise of emerging economies, especially in Asia, above all China, and the decline of the US. He sees the election of Trump and Brexit as a belated response to the 2008 economic crisis and part of a broader wave toward populism. However, inequality is for Nederveen Pieterse not a predetermined outcome but shaped by political dynamics. The agency of the top 1% wealth elite relies on and influences issues such as economic deregulation, financialization, and the remuneration of Chief Executive Officers (CEOs). Political protests were organized by social movements such as Occupy Wall Street and the Indignados in Europe, and found later expression in the rise of new political parties such as Podemos in Spain and Syriza in Greece, and in the rise of progressive candidates within established parties such as Sanders in the US and Corbyn in the UK. He sees the role of the new digital media as inherently ambiguous because they allow on the one hand democratization and transparency, while they lead on the other hand to social fragmentation, discursive echo-chambers, and unabashed trivialization of culture. Yet, Nederveen Pieterse insists that any scenario will also be shaped by the different actors' learning over time.

Todd Gitlin focuses on the specter of disruptive climate change, posing the question: 'What kind of a world can weather climate change?' Gitlin sees the current civilization coming to an end. But how it ends will be shaped by decisions, whether these are intentional or not. The modern dream of calculable futures is met with the uncertainty of unprecedented risks. If human survival is a value foundation, then the search for sustainable futures becomes paramount. Gitlin emphasizes the intrinsic relation between carbon extraction and labor exploitation, yet he also insists that vague condemnations of capitalism are not enough but that there is an urgent need for specific explications of how exactly it fails and of how it can be overcome. To this end, sociologists need to engage more in public debates with accessible language.

Stephan Lessenich questions the self-depiction of Western capitalist democracies as 'open societies', a notion prominently elaborated by the philosopher Karl Raimund Popper and used in contrast to the totalitarianism of the Nazis or the communist-ruled Eastern bloc of the Cold War. Lessenich argues that the mass prosperity, social rights, civil and political freedoms, and decades-long political stability in the Global North is based on the externalization of their costs. These societies – he calls them 'externalization societies' – benefit from an unequal relation in which they extract natural resources from the South while leaving behind or exporting their waste. At the same time, the North imposes a one-sided mobility regime, according to which the citizens of the privileged countries can enjoy freedom to travel across borders while those from the Global South face severe restrictions. Yet, the externalization faces its backlash, as the extraction of fossil resources reaches its limits, as climate change produces disasters, and protests mount against environmental destruction and global injustices.

Akosua Adomako Ampofo provides an African-centered approach to knowledge production. She critiques the Western domination of knowledge related to Africa and the marginalization of African voices. She argues that this domination was not merely confined to the colonial era, when Africans were exploited as slaves or exhibited as curiosities at fairs, but continues in more sophisticated ways today, thus facilitating cultural subjugation and preventing a real engagement with African insights. Among many examples, Adomako Ampofo points to the latest programs on population dynamics and family planning that ignore African views on reproduction but are well aligned with efforts of Western pharmaceutical industries to expand markets for their products. Western methodological individualism appears blind to African conceptions that see personhood as relational and individuals as embedded in larger collectives of receiving and giving. For Adomako Ampofo, knowledge is about change. She applies the notion of '*mɛ san aba*', which literally means in the Akan language of Ghana 'return and get it', to the reclaiming of knowledge as a precondition for transformation toward the futures Africans want.

Turning to Latin America, Nora Garita Bonilla seeks the 'seeds' of alternative futures in feminist and indigenous social movements and practices. Garita regards the study of these as 'undertheorized,' yet holding promise as a basis for a 'new sociology'. She sees within the plurality of feminist and indigenous struggles in Latin America a convergence that points to a 'civilizational change.' Reflecting on several hundred papers presented at the XXX Congress of the Latin American Sociological Association (ALAS) in Costa Rica 2015, she see the study of these as largely descriptive and 'undertheorized'. The title of her contribution and of the XXX ALAS Congress is borrowed from Gladys Tzul Tzul, a Mayan scholar, who claimed that 'we are not a social movement, but a pueblo [community or people] in movement' (2015). Garita argues that Latin American critical thought remained hampered by a still-present influence of eurocentrism and its excessive individualism and abstract, disembodied universalism. While Latin American feminism developed in many different strands and contexts, ecofeminism, communitarian and popular feminisms struggle simultaneously 'against patriarchy, against capitalism, and propose a new relation with nature'. The indigenous struggles enshrined, in the case of Ecuador, the rights of mother Earth in the constitution, and more generally, advanced a new communitarian and ecological vision of a good life. This 'alternative modernity' is opposed to extractivist models of not only the region's conservative types of government but also to its re-distribution-bound progressive types of government.

Asef Bayat engages with the future imagination of Muslims. The widely televised images of Islamist terrorism and the authoritarian tendencies in majority Muslim countries make it seem as if Islam and democracy are inherently incompatible. Yet, Bayat provides a fine-grained comparative and historical analysis of Muslim movements from Northern Africa to the Middle East, South and South-East Asia to show huge variation between countries and over time. While al-Qaeda and ISIS receive vast coverage in today's Western media, their violence and authoritarianism left them with very little appeal among the vast majority of Muslims. In contrast, several Islamist movements have come to accept people's rights and political models that separate Mosque and State without relinquishing their Islamic identity or confining the religion to the merely private sphere. For illustration, Bayat points to Iran's reformist movement and Tunisia's al-Nahda, which was crucial in the transition to democracy and the subsequent writing of a democratic constitution. Islam, like any religion, is for Bayat a site of contestation, a site in which various groups of faithful debate and fight over its meaning, and therefore also a political project for imagining futures.

Saskia Sassen argues that major categories of contemporary scholarship need to be re-thought, that there is even a need for a fundamental 'de-theorizing' in order to 're-theorize' and grasp the 'subterranean trends' that cut across borders and appear at their surface as some of our time's most brutal 'expulsions'. For Sassen, capitalism has entered a new phase. The Keynesian phase that relied on mass consumerism is replaced by a rise of financialization and 'mobile geographies' that move from one site of extraction to another while leaving behind devastation. Technological, financial, legal processes are intertwined across nation-states in increasingly 'complex assemblages' that act as 'predatory formations' and expel people from land, homes, and no longer needed work at escalating levels. A network of glamorous 'global cities' with advanced service sectors, located in both the Global North and South, contrasts the low-wage zones of global out-sourcing. Without belittling the continuing importance of national borders, Sassen draws attention to the strategic programming of borders and the 'proliferation of systemic edges inside national territories'. Specialized knowledges appear here as barriers to critical analysis. Transnational research thus requires a breaking down, or at least a connecting of 'knowledge silos'.

Michel Wieviorka focuses his attention on the role of social movements. Wieviorka welcomes the intellectual shift toward an engagement with 'futures we want' and sees in the emphasis on progress and alternatives to the status quo a complement to the likewise important engagement with evils. For Wieviorka, a historical perspective is an essential complement to sociological analysis. Agreeing with Sassen, he urges sociologists to not only specialize in a 'silo' but to collaborate across fields and languages, and to seek knowledge not only on but also with other social actors. Without neglecting the importance of institutions and formal organizations, Wieviorka sees social movements, broadly understood, at the core of sociology. Of particular importance for research are therefore questions about the relations between the social, cultural, economic and political spheres, and how the democratizing projects from the grassroots relate to the different scales of a global system of nation-states.

Alain Touraine's Epilogue (Chapter 10) is based on his concluding remarks at the Forum's Closing Plenary and engages with the work of Bayat, Adomako Ampofo, Gitlin, and Schulz. Touraine emphasizes human rights, identities, labor, and nature as four key dimensions of a forward-oriented sociological analysis. He argues that no one of these dimensions alone can be subsumed under the others, but must all be part of the efforts towards a sustainable future. For Touraine, universalist principles of human rights are the basis for democracy and political legitimacy. While universalism and particularism often appear in tension with one another, they can also be reconciled. Postcolonial critiques of Western claims to universalism and hegemony have opened the field for recombinations of these cultural and political trends. Touraine cautions about placing too much hope on technological fixes or revolutionary ideology, which can get captured by oligarchies. Touraine emphasizes that liberating change might be more likely to come from the grassroots. His oeuvre provides crucial inspiration for a forward-oriented, agency-centered, critical approach. He urges sociologists to work together with social movements in the struggles for dignity and fundamental human rights. For Touraine, democracy is about creative action. It is not an end in itself but it facilitates diverse actors' open discourse.

The authors employ broad regional and global perspectives in their analysis. None of them treats society as an isolated nation-state container. To the contrary, they see the social as inherently relational. For example, Lessenich questions the Global North's self-understanding in relation to the Global South. Adomako Ampofo's African-centered approach discusses knowledge production in terms of global hegemony, resistance, and transformation. Nederveen Pieterse sees nation-states as major players in a competitive geopolitical field that is simultaneously shaped by technologies, migrations, and cultural flows. Sassen proposes a methodology for 'relocalizing the national' and 'horizontalizing the global'. This reflects the complexity of dynamics on intertwined scales that evade singular theorizing and require multiperspectival approaches and 'transversal' logics (Welsch, 1996).

Differences in the authors' assessments of specific issues are not papered over. For example, Nederveen Pieterse and Gitlin differ in degree about capitalism's capability to adopt green technologies and accommodate climate change. The probably strongest difference appeared between Bayat and Touraine regarding the relation of religion to democracy. Whereas Bayat makes an emphatic case for the compatibility of Islam and democracy, Touraine highlighted the need for laicity and denied the very possibility of a Muslim or Christian democracy. There are countless historical examples of clerics and clerical institutions providing religious legitimacy to tyrannies. Considering religion in terms of interpretative communities, Bayat emphasizes how they evolve over time and in response to changing social constellations. In this latter sense, Christian democratic parties accepted the separation of Church and State as much as the Catholic Church adapted to the modern world with the Second Vatican Council, an *aggiornamento* that in principle can be made in differing modes by any community of faith or worldview (cf. Bachika and Schulz, 2011; Casanova, 2011). Incompatible with democracy is the suppression of dissent.

As the examples illustrate, the authors of this volume do not follow any monolithic paradigm but they approach the challenges of a forward-oriented sociology from a rich diversity of perspectives. A single volume cannot address all the myriad of injustices and risks, nor can it provide a definite list of pathways. This monograph is not meant to conclude a debate but quite to the contrary, it is meant to encourage a debate that is just commencing.[2]

Multiple Futures, Shared Planet

The Forum's motto, 'The Futures We Want', kept the definition of who is the 'We' intentionally open to allow its application to different contexts. How is a 'We' constituted? For the pragmatist philosopher John Dewey (1927), a public emerges around an issue, a problem, constituted by people discussing it. Likewise, 'We' can be a very small group or community, just as much as the imagined community of a nation or humankind. For sociologists, it is not the 'I' that thinks, but it is the dialogue that does the thinking. Ideas are generated in interaction. Yet, the 'We' can be captured as a rhetorical device, creating false appearances of homogeneity, thereby suppressing dissent.

To emphasize diversity, the Forum's motto uses the word 'future' in its rather unusual plural. Futures, in its plural, does not refer to a monolithic ideology, nor to a totalitarian blueprint. No, it refers to the diversity of visions, projects, desires, needs, values, and wants. And yet, we do live on a finite planet, on which today's technologies can drastically undermine, if not even destroy the basis for human livelihood.

The Zapatistas of Chiapas, Mexico, have expressed similar thinking beautifully in their slogan 'Queremos un mundo donde quepan muchos mundos', 'We want a world for many worlds'. From the South American Andes emerged the notion of '*sumac kawsay*' or '*allin kghaway*' in Quechua, '*bien vivir*' in Spanish, roughly translatable as 'good living' or 'live well' in English, a notion that can be traced back to the indigenous resistance during the colonial era of the early 17th century Viceroyalty of Peru and that has become a motto for contemporary struggles throughout the hemisphere, or in Quijano's (2014) words, 'an alternative social existence', 'a descoloniality of power'. The recent wave of protests around the globe challenged inequality, oppression, and ecological destruction, and insisted on the possibility of another, better world. They demonstrate the malleability of futures.

Hopes for a better world persist. Dreams are nourished by courageous struggles from the jungles of Chiapas to the townships of Johannesburg, from the streets of Arab capitals to the neighborhoods of Chicago, from the pathways of migrants to the virtual spaces of new media. Utopian energies have not been exhausted but inspire scholarly innovations. The courageous winds of change that are emanating from diverse struggles at the grassroots call to confront the mounting social and ecological pressures by directing sociological imagination jointly at the kind of futures that are equitable, sustainable, preferable, and, yes, desirable.

Notes

1   Many thanks go to the over 4,000 scholars from 100 countries of all world regions who participated in the Third ISA Forum of Sociology with their ideas, questions, and visions. Special thanks go to the Forum's generous host, the University of Vienna and its Rector Heinz Engl, to the members of the Local Organizing Committee, led by Rudolf Richter and Brigitte Aulenbacher, to the university's staff, including Ida Seljeskog, Frank Pastner, Gerry Schneider, Julie Costa, Hannah Quinz, and the many student volunteers. Particular thanks go to Izabela Barlinska and her team at the ISA Executive Secretariat, to the colleagues on the ISA Executive Committee, led by Margaret Abraham, and the Research Coordinating Committee, with whom I worked on the program. Crucial input came from the over 50 Program Coordinators from the participating Research Committees, Workings Groups, and Thematic Groups, who along with their units' Presidents, Secretaries, and Board Members ensured the overall program's success. Over 600 session organizers are to be thanked immensely for convening sessions that covered the whole gamut of contemporary sociology. Particular thanks go to the delegates of the Research Council and the presenters of the Common Sessions (see Schulz, 2018), as well as to the German Embassy in Vienna for their support. Cordial thanks go also to the many authors who graciously contributed their insights to the preparatory debates on the WebForum at http://futureswewant.net (Schulz, 2016d).

It would be impossible to name all the many sources of inspiration and encouragement, but apart from the contributing authors, a few may be acknowledged in particular: Andrew Arato, Reimon Bachika, Ulrich Beck, Wendell Bell, Alberto Bialakowsky, Michael Burawoy, José Casanova, James Dator, Nancy Fraser, Johan Galtung, Pablo Gentili, Sari Hanafi, Koichi Hasegawa, David Hoffman, Axel Honneth, Urs Jaeggi, Hans Joas, Alicia Itatí Palermo, Guillermina Jasso, Habibul Khondker, Geoffrey Pleyers, Silvia Lago Martínez, Charles Lemert, Daniel Mato, Carolina Mera, Paulo Henrique Martins, Eleonora Masini, Arturo Morató Rodriguez, Aníbal Quijano, Jaime Ríos Burga, Elisa Reis, Yulia Rozanova, Timothy Luke, Raquel Sosa, Elke Ramelow, Jan Spurk, Immanuel Wallerstein, Terry Williams, David Wilson, Erik Olin Wright, Chin-Chun Yi, George Yúdice, the students of my seminars, and the activists who put visions into practice. Last but not least, special thanks for their critical questions, encouragement and suggestions go to Chaime Marcuello, Eloísa Martín, Sujata Patel, and the anonymous reviewers. Of course, responsibility for any and all shortcomings are mine.

2   For related publications covering a yet wider array of pertinent topics, see the WebForum (http://futureswewant.net and Schulz, 2016d) and the collection *Frontiers of Global Sociology: Research Perspectives for the 21st Century* (Schulz, 2018).

References

Amin, S. (1976) *L'Impérialisme et le développement inégal*. Paris: Les Éditions de Minuit.

Appadurai, A. (2013) *The Future as Cultural Fact: Essays on the Global Condition*. New York: Verso.

Bachika, R. and Schulz, M.S. (2011) *Values and Culture in the Social Shaping of the Future*. Special Issue, *Current Sociology 59*: 107.

Bayat, A. (2010) *Life as Politics: How Ordinary People Change the Middle East*. Stanford, CA: Stanford University Press.

Beck, U. (1992) *Risk Society: Towards a New Modernity*. London: Sage.

Beck, U., Giddens, A. and Lash, S. (1994) *Reflexive Modernization: Politics, Tradition and Aesthetics in the Modern Social Order*. Stanford, CA: Stanford University Press.

Bell, W. (1997a) *Foundations of Future Studies: Human Science for a New Era, Vol. 1: History, Purposes, and Knowledge*. New Brunswick, NJ: Transaction.

Bell, W. (1997b) *Foundations of Future Studies: Human Science for a New Era, Vol. 2: Values, Objectivity, and the Good Society*. New Brunswick, NJ: Transaction.

Bello, W. (2001) *The Future in the Balance: Essays on Globalization and Resistance*. Oakland, CA: Food First Books.

Bialakowsky, A.L. (ed.) (2013) *Coproducción e intelecto colectivo: Investigando para el cambio con la fábrica, el barrio y la universidad*. Buenos Aires: Editorial Teseo.

Bloch, E. (1959) *Das Prinzip Hoffnung, 3* vols. Frankfurt: Suhrkamp.

Bonfil Batalla, G. (1987) *El México profundo, una civilización negada*. Mexico: Editorial Grijalbo.

Boulding, E. and Boulding, K.E. (1995) *The Future: Images and Processes*. Thousand Oaks, CA: Sage.

Burawoy, M. (2004) 'Public sociologies: Contradictions, dilemmas and possibilities', *Social Forces 82*(4): 1603–1618.

Burawoy, M. (2008) 'What is to be done? Theses on the degradation of social existence in a globalizing world', *Current Sociology* 56(3): 351–359.

Cardoso, F.H. and Faletto, E. (1969) *Dependencia y desarrollo en América Latina*. Mexico: Siglo XXI.

Casanova, José (2011) 'Cosmopolitanism, the clash of civilizations, and multiple modernities', *Current Sociology special monograph on Culture and Values* edited by Reimon Bachika and Markus S. Schulz, 59(2): 252–267.

Castoriadis, C. (1975) *L'Institution imaginaire de la société*. Paris: Seuil.

Chakrabarty, D. (2000) *Provincializing Europe: Postcolonial Thought and Historical Difference*. Princeton, NJ: Princeton University Press.

Coronil, F. (1996) 'Beyond Occidentalism: Toward nonimperial geohistorical categories', *Cultural Anthropology* 11(1): 51–87.

Dewey, J. (1927) *The Public and Its Problems*. New York: Holt.

Dussel, E. (1995) *The Invention of the Americas: Eclipse of the Other and the Myth of Modernity*. New York: Continuum.

Eisenstadt, S.N. (2003) *Comparative Civilizations and Multiple Modernities*, 2 vols. Leiden and Boston: Brill.

Elias, N. (1987) 'The retreat of sociologists into the present', *Theory, Culture & Society* 4(2–3): 223–249.

Emirbayer, M. and Mische, A. (1998) 'What is agency?', *American Journal of Sociology* 103: 962–1023.

Escobar, A. (2009) *Territories of Difference: Place, Movements, Life, Redes*. Durham, NC: Duke University Press.

Fals Borda, O. (1978) *Por la praxis: El problema de cómo investigar la realidad para transformarla*, Simposio Mundial de Cartagena: crítica y política en ciencias sociales, vol. 1, Bogotá: Punta de Lanza-Universidad de los Andes.

Featherstone, M., Lash, S. and Robertson, R. (eds.) (1996) *Global Modernities*. London: Sage.

Frank, A.G. (1967) *Capitalism and Underdevelopment in Latin America*. New York: Monthly Review Press.

García Canclini, N. (1989) *Culturas híbridas: Estrategias para entrar y salir de la modernidad*. Mexico: Editorial Grijalbo.

Garita Bonilla, N. (2015) *Pueblos en movimiento: Un nuevo diálogo en las ciencias sociales: Convocatoria*. San José, Costa Rica: ALAS.

Gilman, C.P. (1979[1915]) *Herland*. New York: Pantheon.

Habermas, J. (1985) 'Die Krise des Wohlfahrtsstaates und die Erschöpfung utopischer Energien', in *Die Neue Unübersichtlichkeit*. Frankfurt: Suhrkamp, pp. 141–163.

Herrera Vega, E. (2010) 'What is left of humans in a technologically-made life? The relevance of Luhmann's Systems Theory'. XVII ISA World Congress, Gothenburg, July 2010.

Joas, H. (1997) *The Creativity of Action*. Chicago, IL: University of Chicago Press.

Klein, N. (2001) *The Shock Doctrine: The Rise of Disaster Capitalism*. New York: Metropolitan Books.

Koselleck, R. (2004) *Futures Past: On the Semantics of Historical Time*. New York: Columbia University Press.

Lander, E. (1997) 'Colonialidad, modernidad, postmodernidad', *Anuario Mariáteguiano* 9: 122–132.

Lomnitz, C. (2003) 'Times of crisis: Historicity, sacrifice, and the spectacle of debacle in Mexico City', *Public Culture 15*(1): 127–147.

Luhmann, N. (1995) *Social Systems*. Stanford, CA: Stanford University Press.

Mannheim, K. (1936) *Ideology and Utopia: An Introduction to the Sociology of Knowledge*. New York: Harcourt Brace.

Martins, P.H. (2012) *La decolonialidad de América Latina y la heterotopía de una Comunidad de destino solidaria*. Buenos Aires: Fundación CICCUS, Estudios Sociológicos Editora.

Masini, E. (1993) *Why Future Studies?* London: Grey Seal.

Nederveen Pieterse, J. (ed.) (2000) *Global Futures: Shaping Globalization*. London: Zed.

Nederveen Pieterse, J. (2007) 'Global multiculturalism, flexible acculturations', *Globalizations 4*(1): 65–79.

Patel, S. (2010) *The ISA Handbook of Diverse Sociological Traditions*. London: Sage.

Quijano, A. (2000) 'Coloniality of power, Eurocentrism, and Latin America', *Nepantla, Views from the South, 1*(3): 533–580.

Quijano, A. (2014) *Textos de fundación*. Buenos Aires: Ediciones del Signo.

Rivera Cusicanqui, S. (1987) *Oppressed But Not Defeated: Peasant Struggles Among the Aymara and Qhechwa in Bolivia, 1900–1980*. New York: United Nations Research Institute for Social Development.

Saïd, E.W. (1978) *Orientalism*. New York: Vintage.

Sassen, S. (2007) *Elements for a Sociology of Globalization*. New York: Norton.

Schulz, M.S. (1998) 'Collective action across borders: Opportunity structures, network capacities, and communicative praxis in the age of advanced globalization', *Sociological Perspectives 41*(3): 587–616.

Schulz, M.S. (1999) 'Internationale Zukunftsstudien zur langfristigen sozialen Entwicklung', *Bremer Diskussionspapiere zur ökonomischen Klimafolgenforschung 6*: 1–35.

Schulz, M.S. (2001) 'Der langfristige soziale Wandel und seine Interpretation in ökonometrische Langfristprognosen', *Bremer Diskussionspapiere zur ökonomischen Klimafolgenforschung 8*: 1–55.

Schulz, M.S. (2009) 'Structured modes of interplay and the modeling of digital futures', in A. Denis and D. Kalekin-Fishman (eds), *Handbook of Contemporary Sociology*. London: Sage. pp. 291–304.

Schulz, M.S. (2011) 'The values of global futures', *Current Sociology 59*(2): 268–272.

Schulz, M.S. (2014) 'Nuevos medios de comunicación y movilización transnacional: El caso del movimiento Zapatista', *Perfiles Latinoamericanos 22*(44), 171–194.

Schulz, M.S. (ed.) (2015) *Future Moves in Culture, Technology, and Society*. Special Issue, *Current Sociology 63*(2): 127–314.

Schulz, M.S. (2016a) 'Debating futures: Global trends, alternative visions, and public discourse', *International Sociology 31*(1), 3–20.

Schulz, M.S. (2016b) 'Social movements and futures research', *World Future Review 8*, 1–10.

Schulz, M.S. (2016c) 'Social imagination and the politics of crisis', *Sociologies in Dialogue 2*(1): 45–59.

Schulz, M.S. (ed.) (2016d) *The Futures We Want: Global Sociology and the Struggles for a Better World*. Berlin/New York: ITF. [Available at: http://futureswewant.net]

Schulz, M.S. (ed.) (2018) *Frontiers of Global Sociology: Research Perspectives for the 21st Century*. Berlin/New York: ISA Research.

Spivak, G.C. (1985) 'Subaltern studies: Deconstructing historiography', *Subaltern Studies IV*: 330–363.

Svampa, M. (2005) *La sociedad excluyente: La Argentina bajo el signo del neoliberalismo*. Buenos Aires: Taurus.

Sztompka, P. (1993) *The Sociology of Social Change*. London: Wiley-Blackwell.

Tavares dos Santos, J.V. (2015) *Ponencia, XVII Congresso Brasileiro de Sociologia: Sociologia em Diálogos Transnacionais*. Porto Alegre: SBS.

Toffler, A. (1970) *Future Shock*. New York: Random House.

Touraine, A. (1981) *The Voice and the Eye: An Analysis of Social Movements*. Cambridge: Cambridge University Press.

Touraine, A., Dubet, F., Wiewiorka, M. and Strzelecki, J. (1983) *Solidarity: The Analysis of a Social Movement: Poland, 1980–1981*. Cambridge: Cambridge University Press.

Tzul Tzul, G. (2015) *Ponencia, XXX Congreso de la Asociación Latinoamericana de Sociología*. San José, Costa Rica: ALAS.

Wallerstein, I. (1998) *Utopistics: Or, Historical Choices of the Twenty-first Century*. New York: The New Press.

Wallerstein, I., Lemert, C. and Aguirre Rojas, C. (2013) *Uncertain Worlds: World-Systems Analysis in Changing Times*. Boulder, CO and London: Paradigm.

Welsch, W. (1996) *Vernunft: Die zeitgenössische Vernunftkritik und das Konzept der transversalen Vernunft*. Frankfurt: Suhrkamp.

Wright, E.O. (2010) *Envisioning Real Utopia*. New York: Verso.

Žižek , S. (2011) Speech at Occupy Wall Street, Zucotti Park, New York, 2011.

2

Futures We Want

Walking Back the Cat, Positives, Negatives, Ambiguous, Balance

Jan Nederveen Pieterse

In futures we want, what are positive and negative developments, what is ambiguous and what would the balance look like? The theme of the conference was originally a keynote for is inequality (Inequality, struggles we have, futures we want, International Sociological Association Forum, Vienna). Inequality has taken on dramatic proportions. It is a prism through which many dynamics become visible and an indicator of many other conditions.

This discussion is of a panoramic overview bird's-eye character, in brief vignettes because the point is not just the developments themselves but also their interplay and the overall landscape they shape. I keep the format of this chapter light in detail and references, in character with the original address (a wider discussion is Nederveen Pieterse 2018.) The format of positives, negatives and balance is temptingly simple, but, of course, there are upsides to the downsides, and vice versa.

This is a time of major upsets, some structural, others political. A long-term structural trend is the rise of Asia, China and emerging economies, which I sum up as the East–South turn. Technological changes are structural as well, such as the digital turn that brings disruption across many spheres. The rise of social media sidelines old cadres of experts. The gig economy upsets labor markets and services. The sustainability turn (efficiency in resource and energy use) is structural as well. Then there are political changes, such as the Trump administration in the US, which comes with 'a bonfire of certainties' that holds ramifications for several futures.

Walking Back the Cat

The data and statistics on inequality are broadly familiar and dramatic: sixty-two billionaires, about as many as can fit in a small restaurant, own as much as half of the world's population. Breaking news! The number has just shrunk to just eight billionaires (Oxfam International report, 2018).

Inequality has been increasing everywhere. Structural trends are at work that affect the relations between capital and labor, which include globalization, tech change as well as the inflow of three billion new workers from China, emerging economies and Eastern Europe. However, not just structural trends matter but the *institutions* that channel their effects. In fact, inequality has risen most steeply in liberal market economies, in particular the US and the UK. Besides, while structural trends such as the relation between capital and labor, tech change and globalization matter, as well as institutions of regulation, there is also the variable of, so to speak, the agency of the 1%. Particularly in liberal market economies, the US and UK, the billionaire class has been exercising growing influence, not just on policies but also on institutions.

Several ramifications are familiar. When states are captive to elites, people turn against states. The outcome is tides of populism, left and right, which is widely discussed. A high degree of social inequality erodes social contracts and social cohesion. As Keynesian economists point out, it undercuts demand and hampers economic recovery (Stiglitz 2012). It hollows out nationalism, for what sense of a common project remains? It generates multiculturalism-with-disincentives. It produces a sense of globalization for the few, not for the many.

The following is an overview of positive and negative trends in relation to inequality in a global context.

Positives

Majorities in advanced economies turn against liberal trade pacts. Opposition to trade pacts such as TTIP (Transatlantic Trade and Investment Partnership) and TPP (Trans-Pacific Partnership) plays a role in elections in advanced economies. Advanced liberal market economies face income polarization, economic stagnation and political impasse, and have imploded in populist protests, which has led to Brexit and the election of Trump. What has ensued is the rejection of trade pacts that the US had been sponsoring for many years, TPP and TTIP. In Europe, it led to the rejection of reform in Italy and rightwing populism overtaking incumbent parties in several countries.

The underlying trend is that in the 21st century Goldilocks globalization has changed place from advanced economies to emerging societies. This development is structurally embedded in the historical depth of the rise of Asia and emerging economies and the decades-long technological and productivity climb of developing countries on the ladder of value-added in spheres ranging from infrastructure and education to a lot of hard work.

Brexit and the election of Trump are part of the political crisis that has followed the 2008 economic crisis (a delayed reaction in case policies would change, which did not happen). Populism follows economic crisis, as it did in 1873 and the 1930s. A common interpretation is 'The revenge of globalisation's losers' (Münchau 2016). Fukuyama (2016) interprets the turnaround as democratic forces protesting against liberal market forces, in other words, an implosion *within* liberal market economies. The implosion occurs in the two countries that have led the way to neoliberalism, societies where inequality is highest, financialization most advanced and social protection most eroded. In liberal market economies, growing inequality is built in, which undercuts demand, hampers recovery, erodes hope and fuels populism and division. Financialization is politically embedded, out of control and crisis-prone. Because of institutions built over decades, major course changes in liberal market economies are not likely. The spread of options is narrow.

The United States had been preparing and negotiating the TPP for ten years. It is a key part of its 'pivot to Asia', initiated in 2012. Of its two components, trade liberalization and a military presence, now only the military component remains. The demise of TPP is a setback for American economic diplomacy and for American allies in East Asia. The US excluded China from the TPP and its collapse opens the way for China in many spheres.

The legitimacy crisis of neoliberalism and austerity has gained ground. Neoliberalism is increasingly being questioned or rejected also on economic grounds and even in headquarters such as the IMF. According to a paper by IMF economist Jonathan Ostry and colleagues (2016), 'Neoliberalism has been oversold'. In short: 'Instead of delivering growth, some neoliberal policies have increased inequality, in turn jeopardizing durable expansion.' In a recent IMF report on the US economy, inequality and income and wealth polarization loom large as economic threats. In Europe, austerity – originally inspired by German Ordo-liberalism – is increasingly questioned. Germany's treatment of Greece – 'fiscal waterboarding', in Varoufakis' terms – is increasingly viewed as an expression of German economic narcissism. A fundamental design problem of the eurozone is that countries are allowed to run a surplus but not a deficit.

Major social movements find political articulation. Occupy Wall Street found expression in the election campaign of Bernie Sanders. The Indignados in Europe have found a home, or at least temporary shelter, in Podemos, the Five Star movement and Syriza. In France, unions protest flexibilization of the labor market.

The downside of these developments is that none has been conclusive in terms of decisive political influence or achieving a significant turnaround in policies or institutions. In countries such as the US, rightwing forces are way ahead of leftwing movements in terms of funding (including dark money), organization, social media and mainstream media presence (Mayer 2016; Page 2009).

Positive trends in finance. Loose monetary policy (low interest rates and quantitative easing in the US, UK, EU and Japan) that has yielded excess liquidity (in the order of $25 trillion), leads to financial asset bubbles, hampers recovery and finds growing criticism among economists and in Central Banks. It is gradually giving way to a return to fiscal policies that may lead to spending in the real economy of infrastructure, goods and services. The European Central Bank recently argued that QE policies should be coordinated globally with a view to their effects on emerging economies.

The release of the Panama Papers put tax evasion in the headlines and with it has come growing pressure on malfeasance by corporations and financial elites. In 2016 a court in France judging the case of Jérôme Kerviel, a trader at Société Générale (who produced a €4.9 billion loss in 2008) found that it was not just a case of a 'rogue trader' but that bank management shared in the responsibility. In effect, this implies a recognition that bank fraud is 'normal' in an era of low yield. This is part of a wider acknowledgment of bank frauds such as subprime mortgage lending, Century Fund, JP Morgan, the Libor episode, Goldman Sachs (2010) and Wells Fargo (2016, 2017). This falls short of the prosecutions that should have occurred before and after the 2008 Wall Street crisis but it does signal greater awareness of the responsibility of the financial sector.

A significant development, too, is Brussels clamping down on aggressive tax avoidance by American corporations. In August 2016, the EU Competition Commissioner Margrethe Vestager presented Apple with a €13 billion bill in back taxes due to the Irish government. In response, the US government voiced a strong protest, Apple CEO Tim Cook called it 'total political crap' and 185 CEOs of corporate America rallied to Apple's side (Jopson 2016). EU scrutiny of possible anti-trust violations of Google and Amazon is underway. Starbucks and McDonald's seeking tax shelter in Luxembourg is also under investigation.

The hiatus between Washington and Brussels, between what is considered normal in liberal market economies and in coordinated market economies has risen to the surface. In the words of Margrethe Vestager, the daughter of Lutheran pastors in Jutland, 'For all the economic theories and the business models, it all comes down to greed' (Toplensky 2016). Rhetoric aside, the liberal market economy is a world of markets and corporations first. Episodes such as these also indicate that a course correction in liberal market economies is unlikely.

Studies have found there is no relationship between the high rates charged by hedge funds and their actual performance. Many hedge funds have folded in the aftermath of the 2008 crisis and market changes. Other studies show that the link between CEO pay and investor value is 'negligible' (Jenkins 2016), which undercuts the classic argument for high CEO pay – they deserve outsize remuneration because they make outsize contributions. Managerialism and excessive CEO remuneration have been variables in growing inequality.

Global developments. A mega development is the shift from a world organized around North–South relations for the past 200 years to a world of East–South dynamics, a story that is too long and too involved to discuss here (Nederveen Pieterse 2011). With this comes the emergence of new international institutions – such as financial buffer funds in East Asia (the Chiang Mai Initiative, the Asian Bond Fund), the BRICS' New Development Bank and Contingency Reserve Arrangement. The BRICS also plan setting up a Credit Rating Agency.

Of major historical significance is China's One Belt One Road (OBOR) initiative, a broad array of new Silk Roads that include Maritime Silk Road projects. This is a major global surplus recycling mechanism that 'brings half the world together', connecting East Asia–Eurasia–Europe and Africa and the Middle East. It involves financial commitments to infrastructure projects in many countries in the order of $3 trillion. Financial backing includes China's Silk Road Fund and the Asian Infrastructure Investment Bank (AIIB).

China is already the de facto leader of global trade. With the United States stepping back ('America First'), China's role comes to the foreground. China has long anticipated protectionism and stagnation in the West and factored it in by changing its development model (Chi 2010; Guo et al. 2017). Hence, the shift from export and investment-led growth to domestic-demand-led growth and, hence, China's regional turn, of which OBOR and the Maritime Silk Road is the flagship. The US stepping back and withdrawing from trade pacts leaves room for OBOR and the AIIB and gives China greater access in Asia and Latin America. ASEAN has opted for closer association with China (2017). Arrangements such as ASEAN plus Six may now be on the table. China has extended an invitation to Latin America to join OBOR. Kevin Rudd (2016) outlines several postures in China for dealing with the Trump situation.

Global restructuring is on the cards. Scenarios of the late-20th century (such as the Washington consensus) no longer function. The reorganization of globalization has been in motion since the turn of the millennium.

Twenty-first-century globalization comes with pattern changes and trend breaks. What has changed in 21st-century globalization? In short, Goldilocks globalization has changed place from advanced economies to emerging economies. Emerging economies drive the world economy. Asian middle-class consumption takes over from American middle-class consumption. East–South trade, investment and loans are growing. With this comes the rise of sovereign wealth funds of emerging economies and new international and regional institutions.

Developed countries and emerging economies have traveled the path of globalization together since the 1970s, with industries relocating in developing countries, in the WTO, with China and Russia joining, in global production networks, global value chains and Walmart capitalism, but now they begin to part ways with protectionism and tariffs in advanced economies. Advanced economies and emerging economies have come to a fork in the road; popular sentiment and social movements in advanced economies increasingly reject trade and globalization while emerging economies and developing countries welcome trade and globalization. The parting of the ways of advanced economies and emerging economies means that the reorganization of globalization becomes manifest, whether or not it is ready for prime time.

MERICS China Mapping

One Belt, One Road: With the Silk Road Initiative, China Aims to Build a Global Infrastructure Network

Projects completed and planned: December 2015

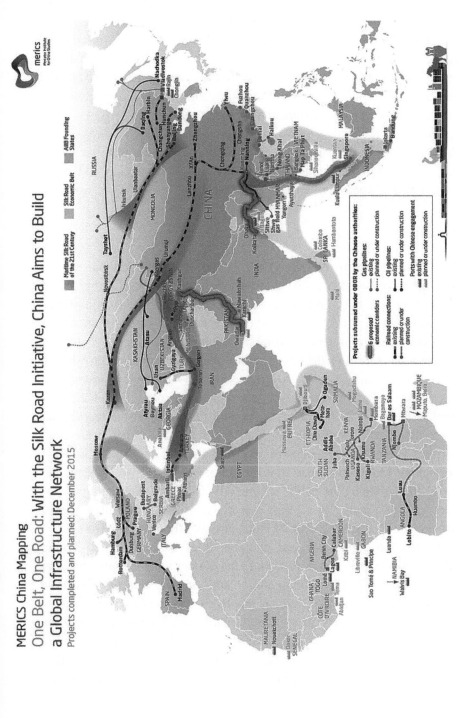

Figure 2.1 One Belt, One Road (2015)

Source: MERICS China Mapping

What has not changed in the 21st century? The weak position of labor in relation to capital (Chhachhi 2014). Growing social inequality (with few exceptions). Financialization and the hegemony of finance in liberal market economies. The deterioration of institutions in liberal market economies. After crisis, the IMF steps in with conditionalities for developing countries. The decline of American hegemony. The rise of China and emerging economies. The sustainability turn. The role of migration as a flashpoint of transnational inequality and conflict.

Path disobedience. We owe Julian Assange, Chelsea Manning, Edgar Snowden and those who released the Panama Papers, and the media that supported them, a major debt for increasing transparency and social awareness and contributing to the public sphere.

Negatives

The Trump administration. As the Trump administration represents a new 'Voice of America', in what respects is it same old and in what regard it does represent trend breaks? It is same old, first, in how this administration has come to power. Because of the Electoral College, rural states and rural votes garner influence beyond their numbers.

Cities generate more than two-thirds of American economic growth and cities overwhelmingly vote Democrat, but they are underrepresented in elections. The Republican Party's gerrymandering consolidates their electoral advantage, which is likely to expand further under the Republican controlled Congress (largely behind the back of public awareness). Citizens United enhances the influence of Big Money. The Koch brothers and the Tea Party are part of this pattern. Corporate media are another major force shaping the public sphere. All of these have been in play for decades. The Trump administration is an extension of all of these trends. Rupert Murdoch links several of them, also as a force behind Trump.

Market movements suggest that the likely scenario of the Trump administration is by and large back to the old normal of supply-side economics and trickle down. Deregulation and corporate tax cuts are classic Reagan-era medication. Goldman Sachs in government goes back to the Clinton administration. In many regards, the Trump administration looks like the liberal market economy in overdrive, same principles, now with billionaires in the cockpit and with aggressive bite. Several of the cabinet billionaires are not the discreet, low-visibility billionaires, but hardliners.

The Trump cabinet of billionaires is a return to the Gilded Age with generals for muscle. It is an entrepreneurial state, not in an ordinary sense but the entrepreneurialism of plutocracy, the state apparatus placed in the service of capitalism big C, with some gestures, partly symbolic, for the economy of Main Street. It is a no-pretense version of the anti-government ethos adopted since the Reagan administration ('get government off our backs'), the tradition of anti-government government, now with gloves off. Appointed to head government agencies (such as labor, education, energy, environment, housing) are those who have advocated dismantling the agencies so they can better implement deregulation from the inside. What institutional buffers there are to rein in banks, shadow banks and corporations will shrink further.

The rejection of TPP would have happened anyway, also under a Clinton administration. The 'pivot to Asia', a position adopted in 2011 with the declaration that the South China Sea is in the vital national security interests of the United States, had two components: a trade agreement and military. Now only the military component remains, at a time when alliances are unraveling, with the Philippines and Muslim countries, Indonesia and Malaysia stepping back.

Is the Trump era 'post-truth'? This may be too much honor. Post-truth has been common in rightwing media and talk radio for decades and entered the mainstream with the Tea Party (or even earlier with the Moral Majority and the evangelicals). Post-truth is also a byproduct of decades of corporate commercial media of a fourth-grade level so a provincial public sphere has long been part of the American normal.

The conspiracy theories in the 'alt-right' go back to the long tradition of the paranoid style in American politics, notably during the Cold War (the McCarthy era, the John Birch Society, the Committee on the Present Danger, etc.; Melley 2000).

A cover headline of *The Economist* highlights 'The debasing of American politics' (2016), but it is the debasing of institutions that matters more. If market incentives lead and everything is for profit – healthcare, education, utilities, prisons, media, warfare – institutions gradually decline. Such is the logic of the liberal market economy bereft of countervailing powers. Weak institutions are part of the slow deterioration of institutions that has been in motion since the Reagan era. Differences are a matter of degree, as noted above, differences in style and tone, differences in conjuncture (same old policies but with different effects in changed circumstances) and actual policy differences.

Two distinctive economic postures or policies make sense in principle. Trump attacks American corporations for price gauging (defense contractors such as Boeing and pharmaceuticals). Both are anomalies in US policies and addressing them is long overdue. They represent special interests that are part of the quirks of the liberal market economy. Trump also attacks offshoring and threatens tariffs on imports, also by American corporations (automobiles and other industries).

This raises several problems. First, trade tariffs intervene in a complex web of economic interweaving (global production networks, global value chains, international supply networks) that has been decades in the making. The America of 'America First' does not actually exist any longer. Second, tariffs may lead to trade war, which are a lose–lose option. Third, these are ad-hoc measures without institutional backup. In coordinated market economies such as Germany and Japan outward investment has been balanced by inward investment as part of long-term national economic strategy. The US, however, as a liberal market economy does not have a national economic strategy. Introducing strategy through the side door as impromptu intervention is no solution. The larger problem is how to manage industrial decline.

The Trump win yields headlines such as 'Trump's win gives prison stocks a reprieve' (Sommer 2016) and 'Banks cash in on Trump transition' (Gray and McLannahan 2017).

American corporations are hoarding cash already and corporate tax cuts adding more, also from overseas, will boost stock buy-backs and CEO stock options. But investment? Resuming the old normal of supply-side economics comes with problems: (a) it has been implemented for decades and supply is no longer the issue; (b) rather, the issue is demand. The American middle class is now proportionally smaller than in most developed countries (smaller than in Poland, Russia and Uruguay; Porter 2016), malls are closing, department stores are shrinking and retailers are folding. The 2008 crash has busted dreams of unlimited credit.

In a wider framework, the Trump administration represents America in decline. The evocation of 'America First' indicates it is first no longer and 'Making America Great Again' implies it is great no longer. This involves two problems. One is a problem that is common to all advanced economies: how to manage industrial decline? This goes much further than just offshoring; it is a matter of competing with new, increasingly advanced producers in emerging economies and developing countries and dealing with complex economic interweaving such as global value chains. Coordinated market economies have institutions and many more policy tools than liberal market economies that enable them to implement more balanced policies – balancing outward and inward investment; pacing economic growth so decline in one sector is compensated by rise in another sector; adjusting educational and fiscal policies, etc. The second problem is American hegemony, a long-term problem that grandstanding cannot fix. American exceptionalism, overreliance on military tools, vanity wars and imperial overstretch are some of the problems.

Different in the Trump administration is the break with the 'liberal' part of American institutions in relation to minorities, identity politics and immigration, in which the alt-right takes a more xenophobic and conservative line. The Obama administration moved the goalposts in identity politics – processes long underway with a civilizing influence but with meager effect on class relations. The administration played by rules of the liberal market economy – markets and corporations first – and did not attack the excesses of banks and corporations (e.g., insurance, pharmaceuticals).

Rickety institutions are part of the profile of emerging economies and developing countries. However, investigations and trials for corruption in several countries (as in South Korea, South Africa) indicate that norms and standards have been rising during recent years, whereas in the United States the reverse is happening and the country may be slipping to emerging economy status (Authers 2016). Several emerging economies no longer tolerate Big Boss behavior while in the US it is becoming the new normal.

Pundits have sternly criticized emerging economies for disrupting the liberal international order (illiberal capitalism, illiberal democracy, etc.), but now an American government changes the rules by sliding to transactional deal making. If the old problem was double standards, the new problem is no standards.

Bernie Sanders points out, 'one of the reasons for Trump's success is that he campaigned on his understanding that millions of working people are in pain' (Taibbi 2016: 46). It is too early to indicate a balance of where this administration is heading. Contradiction and bluff are part of its makeup and a likely course is wobbly. The election of Trump is part of wider authoritarian trends in advanced economies and reflects wider unease.

With accelerated globalization comes a growing gap between the institutional nationalism of mainstream politics and the economic transnationalism of the global political economy. A major conundrum of a hundred years of accelerated globalization is transnational institutional reform (Nederveen Pieterse 2000). Examples are climate change, MNCs, international finance and tax evasion. Yet, in view of the varieties of capitalism, substantial concerted action is unlikely. For instance, an international financial transactions tax has long been in discussion in Europe, endorsed by France, Germany and the EU Parliament (and held up by the UK) but is entirely outside the range and the earshot of American politics.

Developments in finance. There has been a long-term pattern shift especially in advanced liberal market economies (US, UK) from investment in real assets to investments in financial assets. Financial asset investment has been increasing for decades, expanded rapidly since 2000 and 'from less than $100 trillion in 2007 to more than $200 trillion in just the past 8 years' (Rasmus 2016: 212). The shift to investment in financial assets has been occurring for a host of reasons. Financial asset prices rise faster than the prices of goods; their production cost is lower; their supply can be increased at will; the markets are highly liquid so entry and exit are rapid; new institutional and agent structures are available; financial securities are taxed lower than goods; in sum, they yield easier and higher profits (Rasmus 2016). In various ways, this feeds into growing inequality in liberal market economies because it erodes the economic sectors where the majority finds employment and because pay rates in finance are much higher than in other sectors. Part of the background of Brexit is resentment in northern England about London as a citadel of international finance.

Regulation of the financial sector is near hopeless, not just because the Dodd–Frank bill in the US and similar regulations elsewhere are so elaborate, but also because they do not touch on the non-banking financial sector, the shadow banks where the bulk of money circulates. Another dark cloud is the debt super cycle that affects the US, the EU and Japan, which now extends to China (Pettis 2013, 2014).

Developments in emerging economies and developing countries. Latin America sees the waning of the pink tide, with governance changes in Argentina, Brazil and Peru. Military governments have come back to power in Thailand and Egypt. Authoritarian trends are in evidence in the Philippines, Ethiopia and the Democratic Republic of Congo. Governance failures are in evidence in Venezuela, Cuba, Malaysia and South Africa. These concern not just economic policies but also institutions, such as in Malaysia. In the wake of the 2008 crisis, the drop in commodity prices after 2011 and the collapse of energy prices, a host of developing countries have experienced a debt crisis and have had to knock on the doors of the IMF, such as Angola, Ghana, Azerbaijan.

Meanwhile at the IMF, there has been a change in perspectives (allowing capital controls, less enthusiasm about neoliberalism) but not necessarily in policies and conditionalities, most of which are same old. Extensive research of IMF lending shows that its conditionalities have not actually changed over 1985–2014 (Kentikelenis et al. 2016).

Developments in the Middle East. The short story is there are no developments to speak of in the Middle East because it remains in the deepfreeze of history, tucked away there by sixty years of American hegemony, going back to the Suez crisis. Israel and Saudi Arabia, the world's two most reactionary regimes, have shared this hegemony. This alone makes a dark joke of American claims to a liberal world order and American world leadership (the indispensable nation, the United States stands taller and looks further, etc.). What sixty years of American hegemony in the Middle East yields is a war-and-wall model.

One of Israel's contributions to world history is its mastery of border defense tech with a 'smart wall'. Among Saudi Arabia's contributions is its sponsorship of reactionary Islam that has contributed to major setbacks across the region and Muslim Asia. The US has been a party to this because American oil money has enabled and sustained this reactionary pattern, initially with a view to cultivating Islam as part of the Cold War. Hence, Tim Mitchell calls it McJihad (2002). The spillover of Middle East violence now extends to many regions.

Ambiguous

Then there are things that are ambiguous, difficult to place in a box with a fixed label. What about the art of Jeff Koons? Irreverent, technically accomplished, an extension of pop art, yet also conspicuously lightweight, as if promoting the unbearable lightness of contemporary times.

That the Asian middle class takes over from the American middle class in driving world economic growth is profoundly significant and rooted in deep historical transformations. The world returns to its historical normal with Asia as the driver. Yet, of course, no matter where it happens to pop up, consumerism is also just that; second, much of Asian consumption is, so far, derivative of western brands and styles; third, the ecological burden shifts geographically but still remains or grows.

How to situate and evaluate the digital turn and the rise of social media? It is empowering in many ways with a democratization of knowledge and a disruption of vertical expert cultures and hierarchies. Yet, it also enables cyber tunnels and bubbles with inbuilt confirmation bias and propaganda circuits. It also comes with trivialization of culture, which is nothing new.

Balance

Yue Minjun's artwork 'A-maze-ing Laughter' consists of a series of statues of men doubled over in laughter. Why are they so amused? Because the idea of striking a balance among these positives and negatives is too ludicrous and funny. How, by what criteria or methodology, could we conceivably strike such a balance? Are the scales of justice only three-dimensional? Yet, two general points may be relevant.

A classic pattern in science fiction is to show the combination of advanced technology and archaic or medieval morality, i.e. there is progress in technical prowess but there is zero advance in morals, in collective ethics, as if this somehow falls outside the range of the imaginable, or of that which carries weight in that which can be imagined. Here the point of caution is that we should not recycle archetypes, even though they are emotionally anchored in subliminal moorings so it feels easy or tempting to recycle them – as in authoritarianism forever and fascism as an archetype. We must factor in advancement of thinking and refinement of collective behavior over time, in all spheres and domains. This will inflect all future scenarios.

A second consideration is that if the balance of energies now is such as it is, so it will likely be 20, 200 years from now. The contemporary balance includes hefty and meaningful positives as well as negatives.

It includes the rise of emerging economies and developing countries that indicates a growing role of the world majority.

References

Authers, J. (2016) 'Ugly new world risks bringing even US back to emerging status', *Financial Times* 11/19–20/2016: 18.

Chhachhi, A. (2014) 'The labour question in contemporary capitalism: Introduction', *Development and Change 45*(5): 895–919.

Chi, Fulin (ed.) (2010) *Change of China's Development Models at the Crossroads*. Beijing: China Intercontinental Press.

The Economist (2016) 'The debasing of American politics' 10/15–21/2016.

Fukuyama, F. (2016) 'US against the world', *Financial Times* 11/12–13/2016: 1–17.

Gray, A. and McLannahan, B. (2017) 'Banks cash in on Trump transition', *Financial Times* 1/14–15/2017: 1.

Guo, Changgang, Liu, Debin, and Nederveen Pieterse, J. (eds) (2017) *China's Contingencies and Globalization*. London: Routledge.

Jenkins, P. (2016) '"Negligible" link between CEO pay and investor value boosts case for shake-up', *Financial Times* 12/28/2016: 11.

Jopson, B. (2016) 'Corporate America rallies for Apple: 185 CEOs attack €13bn Brussels tax bill', *Financial Times* 9/17/2016: 1.

Kentikelenis, A.E., Stubbs, T.H. and King, L.P. (2016) 'IMF conditionality and development policy space, 1985–2014', *Review of International Political Economy 23*(4): 543–82.

Mayer, J. (2016) *Dark Money: The Hidden History of the Billionaires behind the Rise of the Radical Right*. New York: Doubleday.

Melley, T. (2000) *Empire of Conspiracy: The Culture of Paranoia in Postwar America*. Ithaca, NY: Cornell University Press.

Mitchell, T. (2002) 'McJihad: Islam in the US global order', *Social Text 20*(4): 1–18.

Münchau, W. (2016) 'The revenge of globalisation's losers', *Financial Times* 4/25/2016: 9.

Nederveen Pieterse, J. (ed.) (2000) *Global Futures: Shaping Globalization*. London: Zed Books.

Nederveen Pieterse, J. (2011) 'Global rebalancing: Crisis and the East–South turn', *Development and Change 42*(1): 22–48 .

Nederveen Pieterse, J. (2018) *Multipolar Globalization: Emerging Economies and Development*. London: Routledge.

Oxfam International (2018) *Reward work, not wealth*. Oxford, Oxfam Briefing Paper.

Ostry, J., Loungani, P. and Furceri, D. (2016) 'Neoliberalism: Oversold?', *Finance & Development 53*: 2.

Page, B. (2009) *Class War? What Americans Really Think about Economic Inequality*. Chicago: University of Chicago Press.

Pettis, M. (2013) *Avoiding the Fall: China's Economic Restructuring*. Washington, DC: Carnegie Endowment for International Peace.

Pettis, M. (2014) *The Great Rebalancing*. Princeton: Princeton University Press.

Porter, E. (2016) 'Richer but not better off', *New York Times* 10/30/2016: 4.

Rasmus, J. (2016) *Systemic Fragility in the Global Economy*. Atlanta, GA: Clarity Press.

Rudd, K. (2016) 'Beijing's brutally pragmatic response to a shifting world order', *Financial Times* 12/2/2016: 11.

Sommer, J. (2016) 'Trump's win gives prison stocks a reprieve', *New York Times* 12/4/2016: 6.

Stiglitz, J.E. (2012) *The Price of Inequality*. New York: Norton.

Taibbi, M. (2016) 'Interview with Bernie Sanders: Where we go from here', *Rolling Stone* 12/15–29: 42–6.

Toplensky, R. (2016) 'A career that inspired "Borgen"', *Financial Times* 12/10–11/2016: 17.

3

What Kind of a World Can Weather Climate Change?

Some Philosophical and Sociological Challenges

Todd Gitlin

Ecocide and Exploitation

Six centuries have passed since the British began to extract stupendous amounts of energy from the remains of extinct life buried deep beneath the surface of the earth, placing Western civilization on the track it is still speeding down. But to put the matter that way is to treat 'the British' or, indeed, the entirety of 'Western civilization', as a bloc. 'The British', however, were not all of a piece. Some of the British had the power to convert Scots into slaves. This is the genealogy of coal to fuel the engine of an entire way of life. The impact of coal is widely known. Its origin in slave labor is not.

The mining that started clogging the atmosphere with carbon dioxide was the fruit of enslavement. At an early stage in the development of coal, a 1606 Act of the Scottish Parliament mandated that coal miners be permanently bonded to their masters. If they dared leave the mine, they were considered to be thieves and subjected to large fines and punishment 'in their bodies'. Vagabonds were also at risk of being enslaved. It was not until 1775, with the industrial boom in coal-fed steam engines afoot, that another law declared this to be 'a state of slavery and bondage' and formally abolished it, in part to permit the recruitment of a much larger work force (quoted in Russell 2012). Even then, to prevent 'any injury to the present Masters', the miners held in servitude would have to go through a long and laborious process to win release (quoted in Russell 2012).

The mine owners' new property model succeeded. It powered production and profitability. Mining boomed. A whole way of life built up around it. The cost of coal was low enough to promote its use in heating, industry, and transportation, but high enough to guarantee profits. Over the following two centuries, the principle driving the burning of coal was extrapolated to other fossil fuels, increasingly oil and gas. The dynamic of efficiency was ruthless – because it was so effective, even in unanticipated ways. In the words of the visionary climate activist and journalist Bill McKibben (2010: 27), 'one barrel of oil yields as much energy as twenty-five thousand hours of human labor'. So the extraction of fossil fuels drove the process that we are pleased to call 'development'.

Many feedback effects ensued: the release of methane (a greenhouse gas far stronger than carbon dioxide) from the earth's crust, melting icecaps, ocean acidification, land desertification, rainforest destruction, extreme weather, long fire seasons, and so on. This didn't just happen – it was made to happen, by an amalgam of investment, organization, coercion, and culture. So it has come to pass that the energy unleashed from the remains of extinct life drives new waves of extinction and threatens to sabotage the very civilization that mobilized and continues to mobilize such vast powers – a civilization that strives to be inescapable, to fill all the crevices of the world, continually disrupting and remaking livelihoods, social relationships, and, indeed, the relations of all humanity with the natural world. The viability of this development model is expiring.

This is an old story but it is still our own. It has not been superseded. It sounds the ground note for modernity. Economic exploitation has combined with physical devastation and resulting feedback effects to transform not only the life of the miners and their dependents but the life of the earth. The result is a continuing and unended story of power and profit that offers employment along with unending harm to the miners and the land they have exploited. In his contribution to this symposium of the International Sociological Association, for example, Ercüment Çelik (2015) calls attention to the death of 301 workers at a coal mine in Soma, Turkey, caused by an underground fire:

> The Soma Coal mine, formerly a state-owned company, had been privatized in 2005 and since then was proud of decreasing the cost of producing coal from about $140 to $24 per ton. After the disaster in 2014 it became clear that this was at the expense of the lives of hundreds of mineworkers. Erinç Yeldan, a leading economist, calls the tragedy of Soma mineworkers 'a crime of peripheral capitalism' that operates through hasty privatization and forced informalization of labour.

In other words, the story of fossil fuels is not only a story of investment, and of earthly transformation on an unprecedented scale, it is also, and inseparably, a story of the exploitation of labor. As the anarchist theorist Murray Bookchin (1982) pointed out, 'The very notion of the domination of nature by man stems from the very real domination of human by human.' The wreckage of humans by humans is intertwined with the wreckage of the world even as the domination of nature transformed both human and natural life (if, indeed, the two can be distinguished). The same principle could be – and has been – applied to the industrialization of agriculture. The same powers of control and organization have been at work transforming the physical planet and the civilization that inhabits it.

The result is that, although we are not used to seeing ourselves this way, human beings are now survivors from two time-directions. We are the lucky survivors of our ancestors who themselves survived convulsions – famines, floods, tumultuous weather, fires, and wars. But even those of us who live in the more or less prosperous world are also the survivors of a convulsive future. In the light of the sufferings of those already uprooted by extreme weather, famine, droughts, rising sea levels, ocean acidification, and so forth, it might seem presumptuous for those of us in the more-or-less prosperous world to call ourselves refugees. But we are either refugees from an unsustainable future, or we are agents of change. Our descendants will judge what we made of our refugee status.

Power and Irony

None of this would have surprised Karl Marx, who grasped the world-changing and world-making nature of capitalism. Capitalism, Marx recognized, endlessly devised more advanced means to exploit labor (as well as rewarding it) just as it treated human relationships and the natural world as forms of raw material. It was one of Marx's great insights that capitalists were not just exploiters, they were revolutionaries. The exploitation of labor transformed the material world as capital became interfused with human will. One deservedly famous passage in the *Communist Manifesto* is a tribute to – a virtual rhapsody on – an indissoluble process that, in Marx and Engels' (1848/1969) extravagant rhetoric, performed miracles. It produced wonders 'far surpassing Egyptian pyramids, Roman aqueducts, and Gothic cathedrals'.

This process was, in Marx's view, creative as well as destructive. It unleashed human forces hitherto unimagined, forces that, in their effects, acted like divinities. Capitalists, devising ever-new instruments of production, almost helplessly became the instruments of a process that appeared to transcend human scale. The dynamic of world-changing became second nature to a ruling class of property-owners who poured capital, the result of prior investments in land, knowledge, and labor, into their projects, enabling them to implement their wills and, in the process, undermining the mental and social fixities of the past:

> The bourgeoisie cannot exist without constantly revolutionising the instruments of production, and thereby the relations of production, and with them the whole relations of society .... Constant revolutionising of production, uninterrupted disturbance of all social conditions, everlasting uncertainty and agitation distinguish the bourgeois epoch from all earlier ones. All fixed, fast-frozen relations, with their train of ancient and venerable prejudices and opinions, are swept away, all new-formed ones become antiquated before they can ossify. All that is solid melts into air, all that is holy is profaned... .

But Marx (and Engels) believed the sum of all these disturbances had a saving grace. From a compound of uncertainties, a certainty would emerge. A fever of instabilities would culminate in stability. The proof of Marx's and Engels's rhapsody on the theme of bourgeois potential was already heaving into sight. With the confidence of an Enlightenment problem-solver enraptured by the Hegelian dialectic, Marx saw transcendence emerging from the very bowels of the problem. The developing sum of scientific reason would make it possible to overcome the damage done by the technologies that were, in turn, developed on the basis of scientific reason. Marx (1859/1977) considered that mankind 'inevitably sets itself only such tasks as it is able to solve, since ... the problem itself arises only when the material conditions for its solution are already present or at least in the course of formation.' If the physical transformation of the world entailed the degradation of labor, the poisoning of the atmosphere and the radical transformation of the natural conditions of life on earth, these disruptions would prove transitional.

For all his awe at the immensity of capitalism's achievements, Marx did not anticipate the scale of disruption they made possible. His imagination was limited. Though he worshiped at the shrine of science, the science of his time was incapable of telling him what price would be paid by the sustainable earth for capitalism's achievements. In the bliss of 19th-century ignorance, Marx could not imagine the fullness of a negative dialectic – the undermining of the material conditions under which capitalism had come to thrive. He could not imagine a world in which (in McKenzie Wark's astute words):

> the sum total of social labor undermines its own conditions of planetary existence. There is no longer an outside, a margin, an elsewhere, to dump the waste products of that labor and pretend this disorder that we make has gone away. That disorder now feeds back through the whole metabolism of the planet. It has done so for a while, it will keep doing so, in a sense, forever. There is no 'environment' or 'nature' that is separate. There is no 'ecology' that could be in balance if we just withdrew from it ... So we have to understand, and process the feeling, of living among the ruins. (Wark, 2015)

It must be understood that the ruination of human civilizations is nothing new. The disruption of life by conquest, by forced migration, by ecological threat and collapse, is integral to human history. In fact, what we call tradition is the residue of disruptions. Where there were hunters and gatherers, there was fire. Farmers have known since time immemorial that where there is nature, there is disruption. The Mayans likely fell to deforestation and drought (Stromberg 2012). In the late 13th century, the villages of the North American Southwest fell to drought exacerbated by warfare, with tens of thousands of people migrating to more hospitable climates. The fragility of civilization is an old story. So is the bulldozer jaggedness of large-scale capitalist development.

But today, the scale of disruption is vastly magnified. The nature that disrupts civilization is not 'original nature' – an oxymoron, in fact, according to evolutionary theory – but nature repeatedly shaped, wrenched, and revised by human history, a history that has itself become intertwined with what we are pleased to call nature. The boundaries are permeable. Nature does not simply surround human life past and present, does not simply form the setting for human life; nature is imprinted with human life. Its instability is inseparable from the instability of human life, an instability that increasing scientifically literate populations can anticipate. It is increasingly understood that, as Bill McKibben wrote, 'The planet on which our civilization evolved no longer exists' (2010: 27).

The Modern Present Requires the Future

Thinking about the present in relation to the past and the future entails a break with ideas of historical time as closed and cyclical. The German historian Reinhart Koselleck (2004: 3) pointed to a striking link between the experience of modernity and the subjective significance of the future: the more a particular time is experienced as a new temporality, as 'modernity', the more that demands made of the future increase. Modernity, in this sense, means a human desire to control – as much as possible – the future:

> the desire to control the future, in other words, is inseparable from the sense that the present has a distinctive character – it is not just a continuation of the past – and that it permits a disciplined expectation of the future. One can only desire to control the future if one believes that that is possible. But the advances that are conducive to thinking that the future is calculable eventually shake that very expectation.

Hence two ironies set in with the Enlightenment. The first we have already alluded to: the means by which one believes that the future is calculable are also the means by which, on reflection, it loses its inevitability. It took a long time before moderns understood that the means civilization had devised to extend itself into the future – to control it – were capable of radically transforming that future itself.

The second irony concerns how the future is, in a sense, experienced in the present. It was stated this way by Koselleck (2004: 3):

> if a particular contemporary becomes aware of the increase in his weight of the future in his range of experience, this is certainly an effect of the technical-industrial transformation of a world that forces upon its inhabitants ever briefer intervals of time in which to gather new experiences and adapt to changes induced at an ever-increasing pace.

In other words, the acceleration of time, the sense that world-time is racing, undermines the apparent 'normality' of what has come to be taken as normal. It also makes the future appear stormier. Anticipations of upheavals to come are no longer left to the realm of extraordinary apocalyptic moments – 'end times' – derived from religious scenarios. Not only do climate scientists converge in expecting great disruptions, but so do forms of knowledge and industries dependent on that science. In particular, such institutions as insurance and urban planning adjust to a 'new normal'. Although no particular storm or atmospheric disturbance can be traced precisely or unambiguously to climate change, nor can its magnitude, the increasing incidence of such events *is* predictable. As the sociologist Eric Klinenberg wrote recently (2016):

This current period, which a growing number of scholars are calling the 'age of extremes', has been punctuated by significant disasters that change the way we understand risk, vulnerability, and the future of cities. Superstorm Sandy [on the Eastern seaboard of the United States] was neither the deadliest nor the most expensive catastrophe in recent US history, and in global terms its impact was far less severe than other 21st-century disasters, from the Indian Ocean tsunami in 2004 (which killed more than 200,000 people) to the pan-European heatwave of 2003 (which killed around 70,000 people).

To process the feeling of living among the ruins is no simple matter. Different people will feel it differently, or refuse to feel it at all. But it is worth stating the obvious: that to process it is not necessarily to succumb to fatalism. Sloganizing a response is not necessarily helpful either; so that, for example, one can rest content with wholesale blasts at capitalism without specifying what it is about capitalism that is so dangerous and how an entrenched political-economic system can be altered or abolished. To process is to take seriously the task of rethinking; and acting.

This rethinking needs, among other things, to pursue a philosophical track. For convulsive climate change does not only challenge the material civilization of human life. As the philosopher Samuel Scheffler (2013) has pointed out, it puts into question the values that undergird significant human endeavors. The largely unacknowledged impact of our awareness of convulsive climate change – along with the prospect of a devastating detonation of nuclear weapons – casts doubt on the likelihood of a 'collective afterlife'. Indeed, after the nuclear explosions of 1945, the most farsighted scientists, though not so many politicians, recognized that the atomic bomb was not simply more destructive than other munitions, it presented an even more momentous challenge to collective thinking. Quite possibly, it was this sort of recognition that motivated Albert Einstein's 1945 statement, 'The release of atomic power has changed everything except our way of thinking.' Unfortunately, these words are easier to pronounce than to take seriously.

The eruption of apocalyptic futures within the heart of modernity has been an intellectual bombshell. The dangers are no longer confined to the realm of prophecy. Since Mary Shelley's *Frankenstein*, at least, dystopias have been repeatedly imagined as the products of human creation, not gods wreaking revenge on errant humanity. Posterity ceases to be an assumption and becomes a hypothesis. If artists, scientists,

builders, statesmen, and many others motivate their work with a mind
to posterity, what happens when posterity cannot be taken for granted?
The prospect of posterity is, for Scheffler, not only a minor fillip of
speech but a foundational premise. He argues that 'we need humanity
to have a future for the very idea that things *matter* to retain a secure
place in our conceptual repertoire' (2013: 60). The belief that there
will be a human future is the unspoken core of our values. 'Our confidence in our values', Scheffler concludes, 'depends both on death,
which is inevitable and which many of us nevertheless fear, and on
the survival of human life, which is not at all inevitable and threats to
which most of us do not fear enough' (2013: 110).

If a sustainable future is not within reach, is our humanity not funda-
mentally curtailed? Do we not, then, live among the ruins of the future?

Directions for Sociologists

Uncertainty about the personal future is a human condition, but even as
we strive to conceptualize human interrelations in the light of technological change, collective uncertainty – uncertainty about the prospects for
humanity as a whole – is now a shared fate. With shared uncertainty come
benefits. The collaboration of governments in subscribing to the Paris
Accord of December 2015 points to the potential, at least, for an unprecedented level of shared information and cooperation. The scale of the
danger comes with knowledge that 'we're all in it together'. With shared
information comes shared recognition. If we do live among the ruins of
the future, there is benefit in knowing that others share this recognition
and that a conversation about consequences and appropriate actions ought
to be feasible. Intellectual life is also rising to the challenge. Not only the
hard climate sciences but other fields – development and trade economics, agronomy, and public health among them – are seeking to address the
emergence of new questions. It is increasingly recognized by economists
outside the neoliberal consensus that the dumping of a firm's costs into
the public world may be a convenience for the firm but is blind to the
consequences for the environment – the environment that is not just the
surrounding but the medium in which all human action takes place.

In the necessary conversation, sociology has a significant part to
play. But the field cannot be contented with 19th-century roots and
20th-century flowerings. In addition to opening up new approaches
to a host of classical questions that now emerge on an unprecedented

scale – thus, the study of disasters, the study of the strengths and weaknesses of social planning, the impact of class on natural changes, the study of cultural change – sociology must now contend with a radical change in the human time horizon. Theoretical sociology aspired either to a picture of a single interconnected world or to a differentiating prism, but both models presupposed a future that would be no more than a continuation of one past or another. From such fragments of the past, sociology sought master concepts in order to compose master narratives, but all of them presupposed a ground of values that is now, and for the indefinite future, at risk. It is not that we need *less* theory, we need *more encompassing* theory that not only develops concepts but (1) is mindful of the ways in which thinking about the present presupposes assumptions about the future, theory that also (2) makes contact with concrete problems and (3) evaluates efforts underway to move toward – as well as away from – a sustainable world.

It would be too easy for sociologists to throw up their hands and confine themselves to pursuing more manageable analytical territories – to narrow their definition of data and to demote consideration of any imagined future altogether. But this would be to abandon the idea of humanity in favor of national and other sectoral surrogates. In a world so deeply at risk, there can now be no vision of a human future without reincorporating human nature into humanity and nature simultaneously.

I do not pretend to know how to go about a theoretical reconstruction of sociology. I offer only a few suggestions, hoping only to provoke some thought about territories to open up.

Sociology needs to take account, and urgently, of the melding of social and natural, because so-called nature is social – not 'socially constructed' as if from the void, but nature and society melted into each other. That we live in a Möbius strip world was grasped by Fernand Braudel and his colleagues of the Annales school. A replenishing of the Annales tradition is called for. Social histories need to take account of natural convulsions. But the merit of the Annales approach lies in no small degree in the modesty of its ambition, and this is also a feature to be emulated.

What is more speculative, but no less necessary, is to study the impacts of climate activists, social planners, and political agreements on culture and the conditions of life.

Generally, the study of social change needs to wrestle with a fundamental discrepancy between orientations in modern societies. It has been identified by Richard Flacks (1988) under the headings 'making history' and 'making life'. Most people, under most circumstances, are content to 'make life'. They cultivate and protect families, pursue interests, strive to increase their life-chances, adapt to transformed circumstances. Activists, on the other hand, strive to 'make history'. However, also colored by personal desires, their projects occupy a larger canvas. Often their history-changing efforts begin with attempts to defend themselves – their lives, their livelihoods, their land, their health, their possessions, or some other dimension of their communities – against transformations from without. Their goals may well change. But however the impulse may first emerge, it develops toward an assumption that social arrangements are malleable and that coordinated human action can be effective. To greater or lesser degrees, social movements – as well as the social clusters that give rise to them, the organizations and parties that accompany or succeed them – think big not only about the levers they seek to pull but the larger social machinery they seek to engage.

For ordinary purposes, the close-up time horizon of everyday life is workable. The actions of everyday life deliver results; or in any case offer the possibility of doing so; or offer satisfactions – including the sense of belonging to a tradition – that compensate for the practical dubiousness of the outcomes. The imagination is not challenged to transcend everyday action. They seem, in any event, the only actions possible.

One question sociologists might usefully explore is whether growing awareness of the actuality and consequences of extreme climate change suggests something of a generational transition in thinking about the future. It is a staple of activists of all stripes that they claim to act on behalf of the future – for their children and grandchildren, at least. Is it the case that awareness of future prospects now colors the life-horizons of generations – at least in some situations – in a new way? Who now understands that posterity is at risk, and what do they do with that recognition? For that matter, is it necessary to understand that posterity is at risk in order to take constructive actions? What happens when people who share that understanding try to engage others who do not? What do we know about attempts to recruit climate activists from among populations – for example, evangelical Christians – one would assume to be relatively impervious to climate concerns.

Sociologists can do concrete research that may prove useful to campaigns to change climate-relevant policies. We need to map corporate and state power clusters and networks that presently invest in disruption for the benefit of the property and political interests. We need studies of specific cases where disaster is being organized by the actions and inactions of social institutions. For disruptions are made to happen. Names need to be named and fingers pointed.

But it must be kept in mind that we are not beginning in Year Zero. Policy changes are underway. Shifts in energy generation are underway. Sociologists need to analyze the results of policies adopted – and not adopted – in various countries and regions. We need studies of successful and unsuccessful campaigns to convert toward sustainable energy. For a critical sociology does not stand on an exalted plane and decry the depredations that are all too easy to find. Sociology needs to engage with the practical activity of adaptation, mitigation, and resistance.

Last but by no means least, sociologists need to write in the vernacular. This may seem the most trivial of imperatives, and I realize that I am vulnerable to the charge that, throughout this present writing, I have not heeded my own advice. To this charge I plead guilty, though in my defense I would add that most of my own writing on climate is not for specialists. But even in this chapter I am mindful that the goal is not just to map hell but to change it. Sociology operates in society. It is the attempt to help society grasp its own situation, and the audience for that attempt is obviously social. The levers of potential change are in the hands of human beings who have no interest in jargon or the arcana of theory, even if, at times, it may be fruitful to conduct a specialized conversation. Communication with a larger public is not incidental. It is of the essence.

References

Bookchin, Murray (1982) *The Ecology of Freedom: The Emergence and Dissolution of Hierarchy*. Palo Alto, CA: Cheshire Books. http://libcom.org/library/ecology-freedom-murray-bookchin.

Çelik, Ercüment (2015) 'Mining, labour and the future we want', *WebForum on The Futures We Want*, edited by Markus S. Schulz. New York: ISA (September). http://futureswewant.net/ercument-celik-mining/ (accessed April 2018).

Flacks, Richard (1988) *Making History: The American Left and the American Mind*. New York: Columbia University Press.

Klinenberg, Eric (2016). 'Climate change: Adaptation, mitigation, and critical infrastructures', *Public Culture*, *28*(2(79)): 187–92.

Koselleck, Reinhart (2004) *Futures Past: On the Semantics of Historical Time* (trans. Keith Tribe). New York: Columbia University Press.

Marx, Karl (1859/1977) 'Preface', *A Contribution to the Critique of Political Economy*. Moscow: Progress Publishers, 1977. www.marxists.org/archive/marx/works/1859/critique-pol-economy/preface.htm (accessed April 2018).

Marx, Karl and Engels, Friedrich (1848/1969) 'Manifesto of the Communist Party,' *Selected Works, Vol. 1*. Moscow: Progress Publishers, Moscow. https://www.marxists. org/archive/marx/works/download/pdf/Manifesto.pdf (accessed 2016).

McKibben, Bill (2010) *Earth: Making a Life on a Tough New Planet*. New York: Times Books.

Russell, Albert (2012) 'Coalmining', www.hoodfamily.info/coal/coalmining.html (accessed 2016).

Scheffler, Samuel (2013) *Death and the Afterlife*. New York: Oxford University Press.

Stromberg, Joseph (2012) 'Why did the Mayan civilization collapse?', *Smithsonian Magazine* (August). http://smithsonian.com.

Wark, McKenzie (2015) '(Social) Theory for the Anthropocene,' *WebForum on The Futures We Want*, edited by Markus S. Schulz. New York: ISA (November). http:// futureswewant.net/mckenzie-wark-anthropocene/ (accessed April 2018).

4

The 'Open Society' and Its Contradictions

Towards a Critical Sociology of Global Inequalities

Stephan Lessenich

'Living Beyond Our Means' – or Beyond the Means of Others?

With the rise of neoliberalism in the advanced capitalist societies since the 1970s, it has become commonplace for politicians, economists, and employers' representatives to urge people not to 'live beyond their means'. Be it labor unions struggling for higher wages, pensioners claiming their legitimate right to retirement or low-income households not economizing as much as the better-off would like them to – they all are regularly reminded that the times of plenty are over and are confronted with the public accusation of obviously not having become aware of 'the signs of the times'.

Ideological as the neoliberal discourse of market autonomy and self-responsibility, consumer choice, and (never change a winning story) 'self-regulating markets' might be: in a certain sense the neoliberal narrative is right. Albeit without knowing it – or even wanting to know. Because it is pretty true: the times of plenty are over, yet we still do not seem to get the message. We still think that things can go (and indeed should go) on as they did and as we have become accustomed to. We want our individual lives and our collective life-style not to be changed. We do not want them to be challenged by a social world we eagerly construct as processing somewhere at the 'outside' of our own, as being somehow 'external' to our way of living and working, producing and consuming, thinking and behaving.

Seen from a global perspective, for a long time we have been living, in the advanced capitalist democracies of the Northern hemisphere, in an enclave of wealth and affluence, in a refuge of collective welfare and subjective well-being. Anders Fogh Rasmussen, former Secretary General of the North Atlantic defense alliance, put it in a nutshell when, at the Wales summit of the organization in September 2014, he raved of 'our transatlantic community' as representing 'an island of security, stability, and prosperity, surrounded by an arc of crises' (Roulo, 2014). Fogh Rasmussen and his comrades-in-arms across the North Atlantic Treaty Organization (NATO) or the Organization for Economic Co-operation and Development (OECD), in Europe and North America, have been telling us for decades now that our 'prosperity' is and has always been a matter of the exceptional levels of productivity, competitiveness, and innovativeness of advanced, 'Western' capitalism – and its 'stability' a manifestation of a democratic polity civilized and pacified by means of class compromise, social rights, and economic redistribution. Let's be honest and face it: we all, individually as well as collectively, have been happy to buy this story. While we have reached historically unknown levels of socio-economic development by means of a remarkable display of 'blood, sweat, and tears', so the story goes, the rest of the not only less fortunate, but also less hard-working, and therefore 'underdeveloped' world just lost track and lagged behind. A real pity, indeed – but that's the way it is.

Popular and convenient as this story may be, it is time to set it straight – and face things as they really are. The triumphant model of socio-economic development of the advanced capitalist economies in the Global North is doomed to die. It rested on a dynamic of growth and accumulation that was dependent on the unusual post-World War II 'golden age' constellation of economic reconstruction and cultural restraint (Marglin, 1990). It was built on the systematic exploitation and overuse of natural resources, on the regardless pollution of air and water and the unrestrained congestion of biological and ecological sinks (Moore, 2015). And it was based on a collective way of life, a societal mode of producing and consuming that is all but generalizable. The Global North was able to reproduce its societal arrangement of economic prosperity and political stability only at the expense of others. The North Atlantic 'island's' fortune rested on the misfortune of large parts of the rest of the world – and the distribution of 'fortune' and 'misfortune' across the globe was surely not a matter of pure chance or mere coincidence (Galeano, 1973).

To put it in a different nutshell: The advanced political economies of the Global North are *externalization societies* (Lessenich, 2016, 2019). Externalization societies live off the wealth and the resources, the labor forces of and the life chances in other societies. Part of the Western 'security, stability, and prosperity' story is that people living in externalization societies are – on average and in comparative terms – better off just because people in other parts of the world are worse off. 'Blood, sweat, and tears' are shed in the poorer parts of the world for the sake of our well-being, for facilitating and securing our 'way of life'.

What neoliberals of all sorts do not want to know but definitely should know: 'We', the relatively well-off majorities in the capitalist societies of Europe, North America, and Oceania, definitely do not live beyond *our* means. In reality, we live beyond the means of *others*, of all those 'who labor and are heavy laden' in the subordinated economies and polities of the Global South.

There are at least two major paths that Western capitalist democracies have established historically for externalizing the costs of their societal reproduction and for effectively unloading them on third parties. On the one hand, there is the global constellation of extractivism and waste export the rich countries have been profiting from, through a global system of *unequal ecological exchange*, for decades (if not centuries) and continue to take advantage of until today (Hornborg, 2011).

Natural resources are snatched from the land, making use of pre- or early-industrial forms of labor exploitation and leaving behind a devastated territory (and a disintegrated local community), which is then again used to deploy and store the often toxic waste produced by those who ruined the land (or in whose name and for whose sake it was ruined) in the first place.

On the other hand, there is a *global mobility divide* that secures life chances and extends the operating range for citizens of the affluent societies while effectively excluding and restricting the set of life opportunities of non-citizens (Mau et al., 2012). Whilst we are all used to take our 'private' and 'self-determined' decisions on where to go, where to travel and where to stay, and while the impending suspension of the Schengen treaty is widely discussed as a potential threat to EU citizens' freedom of mobility, this very freedom is being denied, through visa regulations, border regimes, and limits to immigration, to non-nationals whose places of origin are arbitrarily, and often counterfactually, defined as 'safe third countries'.

In what follows, I will almost exclusively refer to and elaborate on this second point, casting a side-glance only to the first one. Actually, both are part of the same externalization story and can be separated from each other only analytically. But in the end, this is what the social sciences are meant to do: to keep things separate analytically – and, if everything goes well, to bring them together again at the end of the day. This is exactly what I will be trying to do, if only in a very sketchy way, in the concluding part of this chapter.

The 'Open Society' – Revisited

How open is the 'open society'? Since Sir Karl Popper published his *The Open Society and Its Enemies* (Popper, 1945), the openness of liberal democracy – to historical contingency, to differences in belief, to political dissent – is part and parcel of the self-description and self-depiction of the Western world. In the times of the Cold War following the defeat of Nazi Germany, it was ideological and institutional totalitarianism of all sorts, but mainly the political philosophy of Marxism and the political system of the so-called 'real socialist' countries on the other side of the 'iron curtain', who were said to be the main enemies of liberal democracies and of the liberal-democratic way of life.

However, under the surface of the 'battle of the systems' and the Western countries' multi-level struggle for global dominance with the 'second world' of the Soviet empire, there was a further enemy to liberal democracy and its alleged openness, usually not mentioned in the Westerners' self-adulating discourse: the poor countries of the so-called 'Third World'. As a matter of fact, the asserted open-mindedness of the 'open society' clashed substantially with its closure towards the needs and wants, the concerns and demands of the non-Western world and its populations. Even more to the point, one could say that the 'openness' of liberal democracy was functionally dependent on building effective shields against its outer world.

It is this dialectic of openness and closure I want to focus on in what follows. Today, this built-in dialectic of democratic capitalism has become most visible and is becoming ever more palpable – for the time being mostly for others. But there is no doubt that the structural contradictions associated with this dialectic are just about to hit back on Western societies, and thus on ourselves. Confronted with migration flows unprecedented in post-war times (Kingsley, 2016), liberal democracies rediscover the idea of the political closure of the nation-state and try to reserve the fruits of democratic capitalism to their national citizens only. At the same time, driven by the habits of prosperity, the societies in the Global North fiercely hold to their industrialist model of economic development, despite the negative externalities it inevitably and undeniably produces for the societies throughout the South – externalities that in turn lie at the heart of the very migration flows the rich democracies are desperately trying to confine and detain. This is basically what the paradox of democratic capitalism is about: obviously living on the externalization of its negative effects to third parties, it is dependent on effectively immunizing itself against the potential backlash of its externalization regime. By all appearances, at the beginning of the 21st century the combination of economic coercion and moral suasion does not suffice any more to detain the external world from counteracting and criss-crossing, underrunning and subverting the global order the liberal democracies have been establishing after World War II. It is now increasingly the military option that has to be resorted to in order to safeguard the political, economic, and social privileges we have become accustomed to in the age of security, stability, and prosperity (Carr, 2015). This is where Anders Fogh Rasmussen enters the scene.

Or Thomas Humphrey Marshall, for that matter. Marshall, writing like Popper in the aftermath of the war, is the author of the authoritative sociological – and, as it were, political – account of modern liberal democracies as the cause and consequence of what he called 'citizenship' (Marshall, 1950). Marshall reconstructs the history of modern (in his case: British) society as a history of the development of citizenship as a social status being granted to ever more people and being enriched with ever more legal entitlements in the course of time. In the 20th century, citizenship encompasses, according to Marshall, civil rights (like the freedom of speech or the freedom of contract), political rights (the right to organize collectively and, most importantly, to vote), and social rights (i.e., the right to a modicum of material security and to free access to the education system as well as to health services). Modernization theorist as he ultimately was, Marshall assumed that the history of citizenship was one of the gradual and irresistible inclusion of, in the end, all the members of a political community into the scope of the whole set of rights being called for by people and granted to them by the state (Giddens, 1982). Nobody would – and, in the Parsonian and later on Luhmannian adaptation of Marshall's concept, indeed nobody *could* – be excluded from being included into citizenship. (Footnote: As long as he or she met the requirements to be recognized as a citizen.)

Marshall obviously was aware of the fact that the exclusion of non-citizens from the blessings of citizenship was the logical – and historical – correlate to the so-called 'universal' inclusion accomplished by the modern welfare state and its constitutional democracy. But this insight into citizenship as being an *exclusionary mode of inclusion* did not make it to the center of his theory. However, the particularistic universalism of modern – that is, national – citizenship may be seen as its single most important feature, its most consequential property in terms of transnational social inequality. Strictly speaking, citizenship is what economists call a 'club good'. Club goods are defined by reflecting artificial scarcity: in principle, the access to these goods could be open to all, but it is arbitrarily circumscribed to and monopolized by a particular group of people. 'Members only' is written on the door that gives entrance to citizenship and the set of rights attached to it. And it ultimately is not the squad of doorkeepers controlling membership at the club's doorway who deny admission to the club to non-members. The doormen are only the agents, their principal being the club members themselves who prefer to stick with one's kind and thus keep the doors closed.

Immanuel Wallerstein, the grand old man of world-systems analysis, gives us a parallel – and yet somewhat different – account to Marshall's narrative of inclusive citizenship (Wallerstein, 2003). 'Citizens All? Citizens Some!' is the telling title of his historical reconstruction of the making of the citizen in the Western world. According to Wallerstein, people who in the capitalist economies of Europe and North America did not have access to private property and thus to the life chances connected to it, indeed organized and united to fight for their civil, political, and social rights, to gradually enlarge and enrich them – and to exclude other groups from equal access to them. Those who initiated social movements and created organizations with which to reclaim their inclusion typically were reluctant themselves, once they had won their fight, to grant inclusion to others. They promoted the rights of the particular group they represented – but were conspicuously silent about, or even directly opposed to, the struggle of other excluded groups, seeing them as rivals, at least as rivals in priority. 'They tended to act as though they wished to secure a place on a lifeboat called citizenship, but feared that adding others after them would overload it' (Wallerstein, 2003: 657).

'The boat is crowded' [*Das Boot ist voll*] is a standard German phrase claiming that the rights of citizenship are a scarce resource and that the inclusion of further beneficiaries into the community of owners of that resource would threaten to exhaust it. Wallerstein shows that in the history of Western capitalist democracy, it first was the (male) labor movement that contended that there were no vacancies on the lifeboat after it had occupied its cabin – and that, after women had successfully challenged the idea of not having the right to join the club, male and female citizens alike and together campaigned against the inclusion of so-called 'aliens' of either sex. For those who passed the line separating citizens from non-citizens, 'the important thing was that there be a line, one that might keep others from passing as well and thereby undermining the newly-acquired privileged position of full citizenship of those who managed to pass' (Wallerstein, 2003: 661).

Thus, the more the notions of 'equality' and 'equal rights' were proclaimed as a moral principle and a political program, the more obstacles – legal, political, economic, and social – were instituted to prevent their effective realization. The concept of citizen has forced the creation of what Wallerstein calls

> a long list of binary distinctions which have formed the cultural underpinnings of the capitalist world-economy in the nineteenth and twentieth centuries: bourgeois and proletarian, man and woman, adult and minor, breadwinner and housewife, majority and minority, White and Black, European and non-European, educated and ignorant, skilled and unskilled, specialist and amateur, scientist and layman, high culture and low culture, heterosexual and homosexual, normal and abnormal, able-bodied and disabled, and of course the ur-category which all of these others imply – civilized and barbarian. (Wallerstein, 2003: 652)

The Global Mobility Divide

First and Third World, developed and underdeveloped, Christian and Muslim, *civilized and barbarian*: the dual categories separating the privileged from the disadvantaged, the happy few from the unfortunate masses, are still in place – and, to be sure, more vigorous than ever. In this regard, there obviously has been no change to the better in the so-called age of 'globalization', a notion that may well be said to be the post-1989 correlate to the post-1945 discourse on the 'open society'. 'Openness' and 'fluidity', 'hypermobility' and 'time–space compression', the 'global village' and a 'borderless world': these are only some of a myriad of catchwords around which political as well as scientific discourses on 'globalization' have been revolving in the last two decades or so. In contrast, the limits to globalization, and above all its asymmetries, asynchronies, and inaccessibilities, have been addressed much less frequently. Freedom of movement has in fact been enlarged in recent times (though not on equal terms throughout the globe) for goods, services, and finance. People's freedom of movement, however, has not been enhanced in the same way. Or to be more precise: it has been eased for *some* parts of the world population – and restricted for *others*.

Israeli sociologist Ronen Shamir has analyzed the dialectics of globalization in terms of enhancing some forms of spatial mobility while inhibiting others as a dual process of the constitution of 'guarded borders' and 'gated communities' (Shamir, 2005). Processes of globalization, so the argument goes, produce their own principles of closure, they are inherently associated with the prevention of movement and the blocking of access. While 'openness' has become the hegemonic narrative in the era of globalization, closure is the dominant social mechanism reproducing, reinforcing, and even exacerbating global inequalities. According to Shamir, the global mobility regime that has been emerging at the beginning of the 21st century is premised upon a pervasive 'paradigm of suspicion' that conflates the perceived security threats of crime, immigration, and terrorism and builds the ideological background for the organization of technological, juridical, and military strategies to manage so-called 'global risks'.

In this process, the borders of the rich democracies throughout the world – be it the European Union, the US, or Australia – have been transformed into a sort of semipermeable membrane. For national (or, in the case of the EU, supranational) citizens of the countries in the Global North it is remarkably easy to leave their countries whenever they want and come back again whenever they wish to. In contrast, for non-citizens coming from the Global South, there literally is no way to get into the social container which globalization theory tells us does not exist anymore but which obviously, at least in the OECD world, has a life after death. Visa policies around the globe and their historical evolution may serve as a perfect illustration of what German sociologist Steffen Mau and colleagues call the emergence of the 'global mobility divide' (Mau et al., 2012). Let me briefly assess what this divide is about.

Tourism has become a major driver of transnational mobility, even more important than labor migration. In the last decades, there has been an extraordinary increase in the numbers of tourist arrivals. In 1950, 25 million tourist arrivals were counted – on a worldwide scale. By 2000, the number had risen to 684 million, and by 2008 to 922 million. By now, the sound barrier of 1 billion tourist arrivals per year should have easily been broken. While shortly after World War II only 69,000 people crossed a national border each day, by the end of the millennium the number had reached two million (Mau et al., 2012: 31–2). In 2015, 81.6 million passengers started a plane journey from a German airport to a destination abroad – statistically, every German left the country once last year, with 20 of the 80 million passengers heading for a destination outside of Europe. While in 1972 49% of the German adults reported having gone for a longer holiday trip the year before, in 2008 the traveling intensity had risen to 76% (Lessenich, 2016: 131–3). Neither the financial crisis that hit Europe and other parts of the advanced capitalist economies after 2008 nor the multiplication of war zones in the most recent past seem to have reversed the trend: bombings in Turkey or tsunamis in Thailand do not impair the mobility of European tourists, but only make them change travel plans and choose another holiday destination in another part of the world.

At this point one may ask: so what – why should this be interesting or worth mentioning at all? The answer is: because major parts of the global population do not have the freedom of mobility that Europeans enjoy without even reflecting on it. And the reason is not (or not only) that an average Turk or Thai could not afford booking a flight to (say) Munich, London, or New York – but that he or she would have to apply for a visa in the first place. Visa policies are the major instrument for regulating and controlling the global flow of people (Mau et al., 2015). The number of countries a German citizen could visit without a visa at the beginning of the 2010s is 129 (only Finns, Danes, and US citizens outperforming him or her with 130). Turkey ranks number 77 of the world in terms of travel freedom (with visa-free access to 52 countries), Thailand is number 137 (29 countries). But still, Turks or Thais are lucky – if compared to citizens of Vietnam (18 countries), Lebanon (17), the Democratic Republic of Congo (16), or, jumping to the end of the list, Afghanistan (12 countries).

The access (or not) to visa waivers has become a major stratifying factor in the global social hierarchy. Not surprisingly, OECD countries benefit disproportionally from visa waiver programs, while they tend to impose visa restrictions on other countries outside the OECD world. What is more, the inequality in terms of visa-free travel has increased substantially over the past 40 years, that is, in times of alleged globalization. Since the late 1960s, there has been a clear polarization of mobility rights, with citizens of rich countries maximizing travel options and people from poor regions being retained in their countries (Mau et al., 2015). At the beginning of the 2000s, one half of the world population could travel without a visa only to less than 25 countries, two-thirds of it to less than 35 countries (compared to the more than 120 countries all the citizens of the most privileged nations can freely choose as the objects of their travel desire). The so-called 'liberal' Western countries have thus heavily influenced the global mobility regime to their advantage. Polish sociologist Zygmunt Bauman gets to the heart of the story when observing that this mobility regime encourages traveling for profit – and, we may add, for recreation, adventure, or fun; in contrast, 'traveling for survival is condemned' (Bauman, 2002: 84).

Externalization Strikes Back

Be it through unequal economic and ecological exchange or by way of mobility divides and social closure, the externalization society practices a politics of opportunity hoarding and cost shifting at the expense of the resources and life chances in the countries of the Global South. Put in a nutshell, the instruction manual for externalization professionals reads pretty simple. First rule: exploit nature, use cheap labor, sell your goods, and monopolize ecological sinks at some place out there in the world. Second rule: enhance prosperity, promote mass consumption, organize 'intelligent' and 'clean' production, and grant social rights at home. And, third rule, see to it that the access to the outer world is open, while preventing it from having access to your own world.

Arguably, these instructions have been followed by the rich democracies in the Global North since the very beginnings of the history of 'Western modernity' (Boatcă, 2015). Or at least since the times of the institutionalization of what the American historian Timothy Mitchell calls the 'carbon democracy' (Mitchell, 2011). It was the coal-based economy of industrial capitalism that, since the mid-19th century, unleashed the 'modern' societal dynamic of permanent growth, the rise of big industry and wage labor, the organizational power of labor, increasing well-being of the unpropertied classes, the double movement of mass production and mass consumption, the spread of resource-, energy-, and emission-intensive 'fossilistic' life-styles. This dynamic was further exacerbated and, in a way, perfected with the transition, in the mid-20th century, from coal to oil as the cheap and abundant lubricant of Western- or Northern-style democratic capitalism.

Today, however, it seems that we are not only reaching the limits to the seemingly irresistible growth and reproduction of this specific model of socio-economic and socio-political development (Petridis et al., 2015). At the same time, there is ever more evidence of externalization 'coming home': Ongoing climate change and the acute so-called 'refugee crisis' may be seen as manifestations of nature and people – the 'outside' and the 'outsiders' – finally exacting their toll for decades of exploitation, obstruction, and abuse of power by the world's happy few – a privileged minority that is not composed only of those sixty-two people who were recently identified by the Charity Oxfam as being as wealthy as half of the world population (Oxfam, 2016). The truth is that, in terms of global social inequality, it is virtually *all of us* in the Global North who are the privileged ones – and who take pleasure in living beyond the means of others.

It should come as no surprise, then, that those others are now reporting back to us, reminding us of their existence. Ayelet Shachar, a legal scholar from Israel, has written extensively about what she calls the 'birthright lottery' (Shachar, 2009): the fact that citizenship is acquired by purely accidental circumstances of being born at one place of the world or the other. While gaining privileges by purely arbitrary criteria is discredited in virtually all fields of public life in liberal democracies, birthright entitlements are perfectly normal and legitimate when it comes to allotting and justifying the access to citizenship rights. Being born in Germany or the United States or in Uganda or Myanmar, into a carbon democracy or into poverty capitalism, is just a question of fate – but one that is absolutely decisive for your personal destiny. When the going gets rough, citizenship rights cross-cut and even out-do human rights. Why should those who drew a blank in the birthright lottery, those who bear the costs of our life-style and who are excluded from the whole range of life chances and opportunities we are simply taking for granted – why should they keep on playing by the rules we have imposed on them?

It does seem to me that there is no convincing answer to this question – at least none convincing to those who eventually have decided to question the rules. The costs of 'open societies' living in splendid, one-sided isolation from the world surrounding them have gone out of control and have become unbearable for those who have been paying for it for decades and generations now. Uncovering 'openness' as an ideological discourse and unveiling externalization as an instrument of power and dominance is what a critical sociology of social inequalities may contribute to the transformation of a global society that is transforming itself anyway. This would be a sociological contribution to what the Spanish economist

Joan Martínez-Alier calls 'the environmentalism of the poor' (Martínez-Alier, 2002): the struggles of impoverished populations throughout the Global South against the threatening and destruction of their livelihood, their natural and social environment, by the rich and powerful of the world.

We may say that the externalization society, so much cherished by the 'happy few' in the Global North, being questioned and seized by the 'unhappy many' in the Global South is a future we do not want. But it actually is the future we should better start facing.

References

Bauman, Zygmunt (2002) *Society under siege*. Cambridge: Polity.

Boatcǎ, Manuela (2015) *Global inequalities beyond Occidentalism*. Farnham: Ashgate.

Carr, Matthew (2015) *Fortress Europe: Inside the war against immigration*. London: Hurst.

Galeano, Eduardo (1973) *Open veins of Latin America: Five centuries of the pillage of a continent*. New York: Monthly Review Press.

Giddens, Anthony (1982) 'Class division, class conflict and citizenship rights', in Anthony Giddens, *Profiles and critiques in social theory*. London: Macmillan, pp. 164–80.

Hornborg, Alf (2011) *Global ecology and unequal exchange: Fetishism in a zero-sum world*. London: Routledge.

Kingsley, Patrick (2016) *The new Odyssey: The story of Europe's refugee crisis*. London: Guardian Books.

Lessenich, Stephan (2016) *Neben uns die Sintflut: Die Externalisierungsgesellschaft und ihr Preis*. Munich: Hanser Berlin.

Lessenich, Stephan (2019) *Living well at others' expense: The hidden costs of Western prosperity*. Cambridge: Polity.

Marglin, Stephen A. (1990) *The golden age of capitalism: Reinterpreting the postwar experience*. Oxford: Clarendon Press.

Marshall, Thomas H. (1950) *Citizenship and social class: And other essays*. London: Cambridge University Press.

Martínez-Alier, Joan (2002) *The environmentalism of the poor: A study of ecological conflict and valuations*. Cheltenham: Edward Elgar.

Mau, Steffen, Brabandt, Heike, Laube, Lena, and Roos, Christof (2012) *Liberal states and the freedom of movement: Selective borders, unequal mobility*. Basingstoke: Palgrave Macmillan.

Mau, Steffen, Gülzau, Fabian, Laube, Lena, and Zaun, Natascha (2015) 'The global mobility divide: How visa policies have evolved over time', *Journal of Ethnic and Migration Studies*, *41*(8): 1192–213.

Mitchell, Timothy (2011) *Carbon democracy: Political power in the age of oil*. London: Verso.

Moore, Jason (2015) *Capitalism in the web of life: Ecology and the accumulation of capital*. London: Verso.

Oxfam (2016) *An economy for the 1%: How privilege and power in the economy drive extreme inequality and how this can be stopped.* Oxfam Briefing Paper 210, 18 January 2016. Oxford: Oxfam.

Petridis, Panos, Muraca, Barbara, and Kallis, Giorgos (2015) 'Degrowth: Between a scientific concept and a slogan for a social movement', in Joan Martínez-Alier and Roldan Muradian (eds), *Handbook of ecological economics.* Cheltenham: Edward Elgar, pp. 176–200.

Popper, Karl (1945) *The open society and its enemies,* 2 vols. London: Routledge.

Roulo, Claudette (2014) 'Secretary General: Wales Summit will shape NATO's future', *U.S. Department of Defense,* 4 September 2014. www.defense.gov/News/Article/Article/603180 (accessed 7 January 2017).

Shachar, Ayelet (2009) *The birthright lottery: Citizenship and global inequality.* Cambridge, MA: Harvard University Press.

Shamir, Ronen (2005) 'Without borders? Notes on globalization as a mobility regime', *Sociological Theory,* 23(2): 197–217.

Wallerstein, Immanuel (2003) 'Citizens all? Citizens some! The making of the citizen', *Comparative Studies in Society and History,* 45(4): 650–79.

5

Mɛ san aba[1]: The Africa We Want and an African-centered Approach to Knowledge Production

Akosua Adomako Ampofo

In his commentary on the life and work of Kobina Sekyi,[2] author of the play *The Blinkards* (1997), George Hagan provides his reflections on 'cultural affirmation and trans-valuation of values', the sub-title of the first Kobina Sekyi memorial lecture (2010: 9). The main title of Hagan's lecture is the Fante proverb '*Nyimdze nsae adze*', which literally means 'knowledge of a thing of value doesn't destroy it', or an understanding of the value of something ensures its preservation. Sekyi's argument was that by accepting the false notion of the superiority of European cultures Africans would become partners in the destruction of their own cultures (Hagan 2010). To illustrate this concept of the transvaluation of ideas, Hagan describes an encounter at dinner between himself and an English colleague soon after his arrival at Oxford as a young student.[3] In the encounter, Hagan asked for a pitcher of water to be passed to him and proceeded to serve himself. His colleague whispered to him, 'Here in Oxford we do not do that! When you ask for water, as a matter of courtesy, you have to serve others before you serve yourself!' (Hagan 2010: 9). Hagan's response was, 'In my culture, before serving others, tradition demands that whoever is serving must taste what they are serving first'; he went on to explain that this was so that 'if the water ... is by any chance poisoned, instead of all those you serve dying, only one person might die. This also was meant to ensure that no one serving food or drink or medicine to others would be tempted to poison them.' His English colleague concluded that Hagan's culture was superior for looking out for the welfare of a community rather than one individual's self-interest because it 'puts greater value on the lives of others as against one's own' (2010: 9).

Many interpretations can be drawn from Hagan's encounter with his English colleague. It is important to underscore that I am not seeking to essentialize peoples, cultures and ways of knowing; our cosmologies and epistemologies are not bound to our DNA. Nor was Hagan's point to provide a hierarchical ordering of cultures, but to illustrate the need for a respectful recognition of the value of each other's ethical and moral principles. We might draw the following conclusions. Firstly, we might note the obvious, that how we see, approach and respond to the world is informed by our environment and histories – in other words, it is context-specific. Secondly, we might deduce that different epistemologies are generated based on whether one subscribes to a corporate or individualistic development paradigm. Thirdly, any such differences should not necessarily determine one way of knowing as superior to another. However, we could agree, as did Hagan's dinner colleague, that, the seemingly self-serving practice of serving oneself first 'puts greater value on the lives of others as against one's own' (2010: 9). This is not to say one way is better than the other since we could argue that deferring individual rights to corporate rights could deny us our individuality and hinders creativity, an ingredient of human rights discourse.

Introduction

I believe we all have visions of the futures we want to inhabit. While our energies may not be consumed daily with the *struggles* for a better world, practicing our craft as sociologists means that, inevitably, we *engage* with explanations for the challenges and problems confronting our current world and questions of the possibilities of an improved version of that world. For Africanists, such as myself, that improved world includes a continent, and her diaspora, re-imagined in very particular ways within global geopolitics that provides a space for our humanity to flourish by valorizing our knowledge. Admittedly, in a world where some may view advances for one group as necessary forfeitures for others, not everyone will share the same visions for Africa's futures.

As people who study societies and social behaviors, sociologists should be acutely aware that deepening global inequality means we are all at risk of finding ourselves living in Émile Durkheim's land of anomie, or what the Akans refer to as that state of loss of personhood (Abraham 1962; Gyekye 1978; Wiredu 1992). This awareness of the inter-connectedness and shared humanity that requires a concerted effort to maintain equilibrium through fairness and justice is reflected in the sayings and practices of many cultures. I refer to the almost universal notions among African communities of individual and corporate wellbeing, popularized today in the notion of *Ubuntu*, a Zulu word that means, 'I am because you are', and that encapsulates the view that our inherent individual humanness can only be experienced and expressed through acknowledgment of our shared humanness. The Shona people of southern Africa are known to respond to the greeting 'How are you?' with the response, 'I am well if you are well'. These constructions set the parameters of wellbeing within contexts that are mutually binding (Muponde 2013).

The marginalized place of 'African knowledge' calls for a returning, *Mɛ san aba*, applying principles of *Sankofa*, literally 'return and get it', signifying a reclaiming. *Sankofa* is epitomized by the Asante Adinkra[4] symbol of the bird with its beak reaching backwards to pick an egg off its back. It is often associated with the proverb which, translated, means something to the effect that 'nothing is lost if you go back and fetch what you have forgotten or left behind'. While often used for cultural revivalism, we can think of *Sankofa* as the important project of seeking, understanding, revitalizing and acknowledging knowledge that built us up.

Disclaimers, Explanations and Conclusions

Although in this chapter I make some generalizations I am not by any means seeking to essentialize or 'other' any cultural group. Neither am I romanticizing African cultures or suggesting there is a pure, 'authentic', unchanging African knowledge system to return to (more on that later). I am aware that as one paints with broad strokes the risks of reductionism increase and I use the terms African/Africana or Black lives interchangeably and deliberately to signify the shared belongingness in terms of culture, history and identity of people on the African continent and the African diaspora that retain salience given today's geopolitics.[5] In order to ensure that the reader does not get lost in the translation of my arguments, let me begin with my conclusions:

1. Knowledge hierarchies, and the exclusions and silences in the academy, including sociology, are not innocent when it comes to the marginalized status of African people.
2. The mainstreaming of so-called indigenous knowledge (for my purposes today, African knowledge) would lead to different questions, approaches, conclusions, and local and global policy directions.
3. Sociology occurs outside the hallowed halls of the academy and these sociological works – from film through music to photography – especially youth new media, need to find greater acceptance and value within 'mainstream' sociology, not just as illustrations or even methods, but also as sites of theorizing.

In the rest of this chapter I do the following: first I discuss the relation-ship between the knowledge industry, specifically sociology, and people's lives, namely the status of African/a lives today. I illustrate this severally; first by interrogating the social construction of development and democ-racy by looking at population discourse and the policy responses of fam-ily planning; and secondly via notions of democracy, good governance and the so-called 'failed African state'. I conclude by suggesting what an African-centered approach to knowledge production and dissemination today might mean for sociology and the wellbeing of not only Black lives but *all* lives.

The Knowledge Industry and Africana Lives

Despite the large body of work by African thinkers (too numerous to list here), 'philosophy' and 'theory' are still constructed largely in western terms within the academy. Further, the popular oral accounts of small communities, including the transformational counter-discourses, largely remain confined to the realm of 'indigenous' or 'folk' knowledge. Although global popular culture has long *appropriated* African knowl-edge from science through philosophy to art forms, including art and architecture, music and dance, food and fashion, knowledge production has insufficiently acknowledged or rewarded the contributions of African thinkers.[6] Olufunmilayo (2016) explains that the failure to acknowledge and compensate cultural flows reinforces and magnifies inequalities. Sometimes even compensation does not redress the injustice.[7] But it is not only Africans who lose; the failure to intentionally incorporate African knowledge has deprived the world of the benefits from the contributions of African knowledge. A young student of sociology in Europe or America might be forgiven, for example, for imagining Fanon was a unique indi-vidual given the prominent and almost singular place he enjoys in the Euro-American academy. Of course, Fanon was an exceptional thinker, but Africa has produced uncountable individuals to match Fanon.

The fact that 'knowledge', that body of information that is known, accepted and applied, is not equally accessible, is not disputable. Indeed, most countries claim to make efforts to level the playing field by making access to schooling more equitable. However, what is less commented upon or acknowledged is that 'knowledge production' is a major global industry, and, like most contemporary global industries, it is often profit-making and flourishes by keeping certain products in, and others out of the market, or, through exploiting the labour of workers in the industry. Numerous examples abound. It has now been well documented that the pharmaceutical industry has deliberately withheld information on lifesaving herbal therapies to retain its market share of chemical drugs. Knowledge production can also be exploitative, whether it is the deliberate use of information to subjugate another group of people (example chemical warfare), the withholding or selective sharing of information (example medical information in clinical trials), or exploiting labour to create or disseminate knowledge (as in the unpaid work of reviewing publications that academics do). The exploitative nature becomes even more problematic when the indigenous knowledge of certain groups of people is devalued and efforts made to replace it with a so-called superior knowledge of another group pf people. The effects go well beyond the loss of income that is impossible to measure, to a devaluing of identities and cultures and the impacts on 'development'.

Admittedly, 'indigenous knowledge' is not an unproblematic concept. In a wonderful RC32 session on indigenous feminist knowledge presented by Bandana Purkayastha during the 2016 ISA Forum held in Vienna,[8] she noted that scholarly work does not generally acknowledge the heterogeneities within indigeneity and presents them as binaries of 'traditional' and 'authentic' versus the 'modern' or 'scientific'. 'Indigenous' knowledge is generally understood to refer to knowledge that is local, unique to a particular culture or society, and comprises 'folk knowledge', and 'traditional' science or wisdom. According to Nakashima, Prott and Bridgewater, they 'encompass the sophisticated arrays of information, understandings and interpretations that guide human societies around the globe in their innumerable interactions with the natural milieu' (2000: 12). The problem is not that these definitions are incorrect. Rather, the problem is that the 'indigenous', 'traditional', 'local', or 'folk' ostensibly come from societies that are non-western, while the implied opposite of them – the modern, scientific and generalizable – come from western societies. Hence, 'indigenous' knowledge is supposedly particular, and applicable, perhaps, for a small Akan group in Ghana, while the theories constructed in the Euro-American world can supposedly be deployed globally.[9] It is true that western education has disrupted indigenous knowledge and it is important to retrieve them and integrate them into formal education. However, this should not just be about sustaining indigenous societies, or rural areas of the global or economic South as is typically the case, but also about applying the inherent wisdom for *all* societies as we consider alternative ways of interacting with each other and our environments. The theoretical paradigms and concepts we rely on are not neutral or benign. They are related to our contexts and standpoints. It matters what we privilege and what we exclude; it matters what questions we ask, how we ask them, what language(s) we employ, how we interpret and present our findings, and the policies we design to apply our knowledge. The questions we don't ask also have implications. In sociology, what is considered as accepted methodology rarely includes the use of so-called 'undocumented' information (read: oral), except as anecdotal, thereby excluding much of the 'indigenous'.

The academy, both on the African continent and in the so-called Global or economic North, privileges non-African voices and Euro-centered knowledge and methods. Sometimes the Africana voice is non-existent or completely erased. Multiple examples abound but I use one here for illustrative purposes. In a heartfelt piece titled 'Sarah Baartman, Invisible!' Pius Adesanmi, a Nigerian scholar of Literature and French, produces a fictitious letter written by Sarah (also Saartjie and Sara) Baartman to Sandra Gilbert and Susan Gubar, who produced the 2007 *Norton Anthology of Literature by Women* (2007). Sarah Baartman was the most famous of at least two Khoikhoi women who were forcibly taken to Europe and exhibited as curiosities in the 19th-century under the now discredited name 'Hottentot Venus'.[10] African feminists have used her story to draw attention to the double burdens of sexism and racism endured by Black women via the voyeuristic European gaze. In his piece, Adesanmi (via Baartman) laments the 'excision of African theories and theorists' (2011: 109) from this 2,452-page 2-volume collection. By using Baartman to discuss the 'excision' of Black women's literature, Adesanmi makes the argument that Black bodies are doubly abused, first physically, and then through the erasure of their stories. The survivors do not get to mourn and the abusers can avoid blame, guilt and restitution. Reflections on, and critiques of such 'excisions' have been described by some scholars from the Global North as mere 'protest literature'. Calls by Africana scholars for a decolonization of the academy, and knowledge production more broadly, have been viewed as the tantrums of an elite band of Black scholars who are resentful that their work doesn't garner the same reach as Euro-American colleagues. The reality is that the status of African lives, whether on the continent or in the diaspora, cannot be divorced from what is valorized as knowledge and influences policy and popular culture.

As pointed out during one of the common sessions during the 2016 ISA Forum delivered by Rhoda Reddock,[11] the ISA's own list of 'Books of the Century' is telling in the absence of African, and Black sociologists generally. For example, whereas Max Weber appears 14 times, W.E.B Du Bois appears twice. Patricia Hill Collins work on Black feminist thought is absent, although admittedly the list is very thin on works by feminist sociologists in general. I was unable to find a single African sociologist.[12] I am sure there was an 'objective' method that led to the result – but my question would be whose objectivity? The frequency of citations is a heavily-relied upon method to valorize academic work – but the vicious circle should be obvious: if 'indigenous' knowledge is not valorized, it will not be cited, if not cited it will not be used in successive research, if not used its universal applicability cannot be tested, and so forth.

To make my case for the relationship between knowledge production, its (de)valorization, and the status of African lives I will interrogate notions of development, via population dynamics and the policy response of family planning; and notions of democracy, via the so-called 'failed African state'. There have been and continue to be numerous critiques of development, globalization and neoliberalism arguing, severally, that the implicit idea that the fruits of development look a certain way, and are achieved through a particular trajectory persist even though the reality is at odds with this. Theories of population dynamics popular in the 1970s through the 1990s, with attendant World Fertility and Demographic and Health surveys are back on the agenda – not only as an accessory to sexual and reproductive health and rights, but as an explicit field of action in development cooperation (Bendix and Schultz 2015). The theories that inform the policy makers, who in turn design the policies, that are then adopted by politicians, are constructed by sociologists and demographers. A brief re-cap of the trajectory of thinking and policy is in order here (see Adomako Ampofo 2004):

- During the 1960s and 1970s large families among the poor and so-called Third World countries were seen as imposing severe burdens on society, including being viewed as a security challenge. The discourse centered on the 'costs' and 'benefits' of children. Population policies that overtly promoted 'family planning' were the response.[13]
- The programmatic priorities focused on technical solutions, especially the provision of contraceptives to women, who, in surveys often showed a discrepancy between the number of children they 'wanted' and the number of children they gave birth to.

- 'Population dynamics' constructed countries as 'good' and 'bad' in terms of population growth and birth rates. So, for example, Ethiopia has been viewed as a 'good' country for the large-scale adoption of long-term contraception and Ghana as a 'bad' country for failing to successfully do same.[14]
- Perhaps not surprisingly, since it is women who give birth to children, they became easy targets for fertility reduction efforts, particularly because surveys showed that they indicated they were having more children than they wanted to have ('unwanted births'), or they were having children before they were ready ('mistimed births'). Since modern contraceptives can solve the problem of 'unwanted' or 'mistimed' births (both of which are considered as unplanned), women who do not want children *but* are not using contraceptives are deemed to have an 'unmet need' (for contraception).[15] This led to the initial exclusion of men and infantalizing of African women for failing to do what was 'rational', i.e use contraceptives.
- African sociologists and demographers pointed to the absurdity of focusing on women and several studies addressed a 'male role' (see work by Adomako Ampofo, Dodoo, Ezeh to name a few).
- By the end of the century family planning was on the back burner and did not reappear as a major policy and programmatic issue until the mid 2000s, with active 'support' from the UNFPA and the Bill and Melinda Gates foundation.

There are simply too many aspects of the social lives of African women and men that were, and continue to be, ignored to discuss in detail here. Needless to say, however, women don't have children alone, and both husbands and the extended families have a say, or at least an interest, in childbearing decisions. Further, the value of children is not only about 'costs' and 'benefits', but also about the continuation of the lineage, and no child is really 'unwanted' even if her or his arrival comes with some 'inconvenience'.[16] Another caveat that cannot be ignored is the huge profits that accrue to European and American pharmaceutical companies for the production and sale of contraceptives. Writing on the German context, Bendix and Schultz state, 'Population dynamics' have become the new 'cross-cutting issue' and the German Federal Ministry for Economic Cooperation and Development (BMZ) considers itself to be the 'European vanguard' in this realm' (2015: no page). They note that German development cooperation resulted in €169 million being spent on population programmes in 2012, far more than it spent on basic health care (€147 million), and with almost half (€83 million) going to African countries. More interesting is how the 'need' in Africa opened the door for new markets in Europe and the United States. According to Bendix and Schultz, the market for contraceptives was US$11.2 billion in 2008 and was estimated to rise to US$14.5 billion in 2016. Market leaders are Bayer (with annual revenues of US$3 billion), Tevat (US$1.2 billion) and Merck & Co (US$1 billion). The UNFPA and USAID are said to be the biggest buyers for international aid programs, with a strong emphasis on long-term contraceptives such as implants. Thus, poor African women with an 'unmet need' are big business for pharmaceuticals and international NGOs, without any scrutiny of the theory underlying these conclusions, let alone the physiological effects of long-term contraceptives.

The second issue I turn to are notions of 'democracy' and good 'governance', and their association with development. Democracy purportedly 'for the people by the people', includes elections (preferably multi-party) and universal suffrage. Max Weber argues that a state that can maintain a monopoly on the use of force, through the armed forces, police and other state institutions, is 'successful' while one that is unable to maintain control over other internal groups (in today's parlance, paramilitary groups such as terrorist organizations and warlords) is 'unsuccessful' or has failed. Stable democracies do not 'fail'. Yet while there is no consensus on the term 'failed state' this does not keep media houses from using it liberally to construct Africa. A 2013 edition of *Business Insider*, for example, has a list of 25 failed states, of which 18 are in Africa, including Liberia, Uganda, Ethiopia, Kenya and Côte d'Ivoire. Some scholars argue that democracy, as constructed, is alien to 'African cultures', that it is an instrument of continuous exploitation by the west (Morrow 1998; Owolabi 1999), and that we should have an 'indigenous' African democracy (Ademola 2009; Oyekan 2009), which might, for example, be built on the consensus-building model. Asumah makes a case for what he refers to as multicultural and relational democracy – transcending the procedural, where the people's 'engagement and connection with their representatives are primordial, constant and continuing' (Asumah and Nagel 2014: 407). And yet, in discussions, examples and policy interventions regarding democracy, good governance and failed states the voices and perspectives of African people and their academics are all too frequently absent.

Today, the Black Lives Matter (BLM) and Rhodes Must Fall movements (RMF) have focused attention on the status of Africana or Black (and Brown) lives: both are anti-colonial movements, the former focusing more on civil rights, the latter on decolonizing knowledge and the academy (Adomako Ampofo 2016). What is interesting for me as a sociologist are the number of studies emerging that claim either no evidence of differences in police shootings by race in the US, or showing how many white deaths result from police shootings. Small qualitative studies are ignored and so-called anecdotal evidence is dismissed. The sociological imperative to contextualize and measure controlling for region, population size, poverty and unemployment is largely ignored. Asking for an historical contextualization that references the US's brutal slave past, and an acknowledgment that not too long ago law enforcement officers even belonged to the Ku Klux Klan, may not be 'objective' enough.

The BLM and RMF campaigns did not start with the incensed responses to the killings of black people in the US or the frustrations of South African youth with their educational system. 'Black lives matter' movements under different names have been a feature of anti-slavery, anti-colonialism, civil rights and anti-neo-colonialism movements. The response, 'All lives matter' to the cry, 'Black lives matter!' – which of course they do, and which true human could disagree? – reflects many things, among them a failure to understand and contextualize the status of Black lives today, both in the US, on the continent and elsewhere. Further, there is a failure to recognize that by repeating 'all lives matter' one asserts that some lives do matter less. This failure is not only the fault of inaccurate media portrayals, but also inadequate social science research: the questions asked and not asked; the methods employed and conclusions reached; and of course, whose research reaches the media.

An African-Centered Approach to Knowledge Production and the Africa We Want

From Kwame Nkrumah, Leopold Senghor, Du Bois, Maya Angelou and their peers, to numerous scholars today such as feminist sociologists Patricia Hill Collins, African thinkers have insisted that there is, indeed, an 'African/a-centered' approach to knowledge production, and an African-centered sociology that provides a realistic framework for the analysis of African social lives (Caroll 2014). This belief is perhaps reflected best in the exhortation given to the Fellows of the Institute of African Studies at the University of Ghana at its formal opening in 1962 by our first president, Kwame Nkrumah:

> One essential function of this Institute must surely be to study the history, culture and institutions, languages and arts of Ghana and of Africa in new African-centred ways – in entire freedom from the propositions and presuppositions of the colonial epoch, and from the distortions of those Professors and Lecturers who continue to make European studies of Africa the basis of this new assessment. By the work of this Institute, we must

re-assess and assert the glories and achievements of our African past and
inspire our generation, and succeeding generations, with a vision of a better
future. But you should not stop here. Your work must also include a study
of the origins and culture of peoples of African descent in the Americas and
the Caribbean, and you should seek to maintain close relations with their
scholars so that there may be cross fertilisation between Africa and those
who have their roots in the African past. (Nkrumah 1963)

'*Wo nyim adze won sae ade*' – 'if you know a thing of value you do not
destroy it'. Indeed, if that valuable item is lost the one who understands
its values goes back to find it, almost engaging in a revival of sorts and a
practice of principles of *Sankofa. Mɛ san aba*, literally, 'I will return' or,
'I will be back', is the title of a hiplife[17] song by a duo *Akyeame*, plural of
Ɔkyeame, the Akan title for the advisor and spokesperson of the king.[18] By
calling themselves *Akyeame* the duo speak to the notion that young people
can be (wise) advisors. Further, the title and lyrics of the song articulate
the idea that Ghanaians (Africans) can revive a cultural project that speaks
to their identities and needs, including a shared humanity. The song, and
the hiplife style that uses traditional overtures, and mixtures of Ghanaian
languages and English, speaks to this eclectic mix that forms the identities
of today's youth. '*Mɛ san aba*' can also be read as the threat, 'just you
wait, I'll be back to deal with you!' that informs much of civil society's
language, especially in social media, as it engages with the state's failure
to deliver on the promises of 'development'.

Ingredients of an African-centered approach, not to be confused by an
African approach, puts the impact on Africana lives at the center, irre-
spective of whether the sociologist is African, African-based, African
diaspora-based, or not African at all. However, it must be culturally
grounded in a sociological imagination that understands African lives and
relates the field of sociology to an 'understanding of the Black condition
which will ultimately be applied in some effective way to the resolution of
the oppressed condition of the masses of Black folk' (Caroll 2014: 261–2). It
must be developed out of an African cosmology, ontology, axiology and
epistemology. An African-centered sociology needs to tackle the knowledge hegemony intentionally. It must:

- Be transformative and lead students to look at structures that undermine
  African societies.
- Recognize the diversity of African/a and Black experiences within shared
  histories and contemporary realities.

- Conceptualize and explain African experiences.
- Recognize the relationships among our realities (i.e. use an intersectional lens).
- Actively pursue reciprocity and decry voyeurisms.
- Engage youth voices.
- Develop tools and methodologies relevant to African contexts.

This last point is critical if we are to avoid merely doing an African sociology and not an African-centered one. Mixed methods and sources should be valued and accepted. Utilizing 'undocumented' knowledge such as oral traditions should be valued and accepted. Citing Curry, Caroll adds that an African-centered knowledge production within African-centered sociology has no disinterested participants. There is an agenda and we should demand active engagement with the phenomena under investigation from sociologists. This would preclude the voyeur or mere theory-builder. 'No longer can the sociologically-minded researcher be detached from that which s/he is investigating; we must be active participants who knowingly and willingly divulge our role as interested scholars, committed to the development of liberatory knowledge (Caroll 2014: 265).

The imperatives and possibilities for that common agenda among African-centered sociologists must include emerging sites of knowledge production. It must also of necessity prioritize engagement with the youth for the sake of knowledge building and sustenance. More than any other global community, I think, our relevance as academics can only be sustained as we re-birth our intellectual DNA and humanity in the next generation of thinkers. And many of these thinkers, as of old, ply their trade and share their knowledge outside the walls of the academy and often in the spaces of popular culture.

Ultimately, all lives will only matter when we recognize our shared humanity. The renowned Ghanaian philosophers Gyekye and Wiredu – both Akans – have engaged in interesting debates about Akan notions of personhood. While there are important differences, there are sufficient convergences between them for us to draw conclusions about the implications of Akan conceptions of personhood and the relationship between individuals and the community, and the understanding of responsibilities and freedoms. Ajume Wingo (2008) points out that the debate between Wiredu and Gyekye provides insights regarding not just the substance of the conception of personhood (humanness), but also the way empirical evidence can be used to inform philosophical analysis. In this case, the Akan view of personhood has, like many other metaphysical and moral conceptions, far-reaching effects on social practices and institutions. For example, the saying '*Boa me na men boa wo*', literally 'help me and I will help you', signifies co-dependence and the saying that '*Mre dane*', literally 'situations change', underscores the role of giving and receiving in everyone's life. Thus, as Azibo argues (1999), our social theory must refer to 'those principles that determine the relationship of a people to one another, to other humans, and to nature'. In this way, our social theory can establish 'guidelines of life including their values, rituals and ways of dealing with 'the other' (1999: 1).

Notes

1 Literal meaning in Akan: 'I shall return'.

2 William Essuman Gwira-Sekyi popularly known as Kobina Sekyi (1892–1956), was a Cape Coast lawyer, writer, last president of the Aborigines Rights Protection Society, executive member of the National Congress of British West Africa and member of the Coussey Committee for constitutional change that finally paved the way for the independence of Ghana. He was keenly aware of the dissonance that a European education can create for an African. In the satire *The Blinkards* he creates Mrs Brɔfosɛm (literally Mrs 'behaves like a white person') and her counterpoint Mr Onyimdze, a British-trained lawyer who privileges African ways and serves as Sekyi's voice.

3 Hagan does not provide a date but based on his CV it must have been sometime in the late 1960s to early 1970s.

4 Andrika symbols can also be found among the Baouie of Côte d'Ivoire.

5 In their report on a 2013 survey of Black Studies, Abdul Alkalimat et al. pointed out that 'Black was capitalized as it was the assumed name of a nationality', and added that 'this practice continues to make sense given the reality of racism in the USA' (2013).

6 The lawsuit about the song 'The Lion Sleeps Tonight' is a good example. In this case the Zulu musician Solomon Linda received little compensation for his song 'Mbube', recorded in 1939 under the South African Gallo Record Company. Linda's song became 'The Lion Sleeps Tonight', a global pop classic that has generated millions of dollars for others (see Olufunmilayo 2016 for a recent discussion). An earlier popular example could be the work of the artist Pablo Picasso.

7 When Linda died in 1962 he had been unable to leave enough behind for his widow to be able to purchase a gravestone. His daughter apparently died of AIDS-related illness in 2001 because she was unable to afford antiretroviral medication (Olufunmilayo 2016).

8 Research Committee on Women and Society Session 374 'Knowledge Production: Feminist Perspectives in the 21st Century'.

9 In 1993 the United Nations proposed a working definition that 'Indigenous communities, peoples and nations are those which, having a historical continuity with pre-invasion and pre-colonial societies that developed on their territories, consider themselves distinct from other sectors of societies now prevailing in those territories, or parts of them. They form at present non-dominant sectors of society and are determined to preserve, develop and transmit to future generations their ancestral territories, and

their ethnic identity, as the basis of their continued existence as peoples, in accordance with their own cultural patterns, social institutions and legal systems' (for details of the Martinez Cobo study which formulated the definition, see www.un.org/development/desa/indigenouspeoples/about-us.html). This definition has since been vigorously debated and refined in relation to the many different people groups around the world who wish to be recognized as such.

10 See Maseko (1998), Qureshi (2004), Strother (1999), Willis (2010).

11 Her paper at Common Session 2A of the 2012 ISA Forum on 'The Futures We Want: Global Sociology and the Struggles for a Better World' was titled 'Sociology, Feminisms and the Global South: Back to the Future'.

12 I scanned for familiar sociologists and unfamiliar ones with 'African sounding' names. Thus I concede the list might include some European-descended Africans I am unfamiliar with. While I would not attempt a who-is-who in 'African sociology' here, a useful source is the *African Sociological Review* published by CODESRIA.

13 During Henry Kissinger's tenure as Secretary of State in the US (1972–77), there existed a panic around the security of the US if African and other so-called developing country populations were allowed to grow in an uncontrolled manner. The concerns were so strong that the US had a distinct policy to strongly export population programmes to African governments, and also to offer scholarships to African students to study demography at prestigious US institutions. The US, Kissinger counseled, could minimize charges of an imperialist motive behind its support of population activities in developing nations by 'repeatedly asserting that such support derives from a concern with (a) the rights of the individual couple to determine freely and responsibly their number and spacing of children … and (b) the fundamental social and economic development of poor countries' (cited in Mumford 1994: 146).

14 Personal communication, Dr Kwame Ampofo, Technical Adviser, Engender Health Ghana.

15 See Adomako Ampofo (2004) for a critical discussion of the concept of 'unmet need' including some of the conceptual and methodological challenges involved in its measurement.

16 I don't imply that a pregnancy is always heralded with joy or acceptance. Indeed, women do seek abortions for pregnancies that arrive at the 'wrong time' or with the 'wrong partner'. What I argue is that the notion of 'unwantedenss' of a child is not to be taken for granted for many since God gives children and the lineage will surely want them.

17 Hiplife is a combination of hiphop, rap and traditional Ghanaian highlife music.

18 *Ɔkyeame* has often been inappropriately translated into English as 'linguist'.

References

Abraham, William (1962) *The Mind of Africa*. Chicago: Chicago University Press.

Alkilimat, Abdul, et al. (2013) *African American Studies 2013: A Nation Web-Based Survey*. University of Illinois at Urbana-Champaign Department of African American Studies. http://afro.illinois.edu (accessed 2 November 2015).

Ademola, K.F. (2009) 'Towards an African theory of democracy', *Journal of the Philosophical Association of Kenya 1*(1): 101–26.

Adesanmi, Pius (2011) *You're Not a Country, Africa*. New York: Penguin.

Adomako Ampofo, Akosua (2004) *'"By God's Grace I had a boy"*. Whose "unmet need" and "dis/agreement" about childbearing among Ghanaian couples'. In Signe Arnfred (ed.), *Thinking Sexualities in Contexts of Gender*. Uppsala: Nordic Africa Institute. pp. 115–34.

Adomako Ampofo, Akosua (2016) '*Re*-viewing studies on Africa, #Black Lives Matter, and envisioning the future of African Studies', *African Studies Review 59*(2): 7–27.

Asumah, Seth and Nagel, Mechthild (2014) *Diversity, Social Justice, and Inclusive Excellence: Transdisciplinary and Global Perspectives*. Albany: SUNY Press.

Azibo D.A. (1999) 'Africentric conceptualizing as the pathway to African liberation', *International Journal of Africana Studies 5*: 1–31.

Bendix, Daniel and Schultz, Susanne (2015) 'Bevölkerungspolitik reloaded: Zwischen BMZ und Bayer', *Peripherie, 3*: S.447–68. https://doi.org/10.3224/peripherie. v35i140.22998 (accessed April 2018).

Business Insider (2013) 'The 25 most failed states on Earth'. www.businessinsider.com/ the-25-most-failed-states-on-earth-2013-6# (accessed April 2018).

Caroll, Karanja Keita (2014) 'An introduction to African-centered sociology: Worldview, epistemology, and social theory', *Critical Sociology 40*(2): 257–70.

Gilbert, Sandra and Gubar, Susan (2007) *Norton Anthology of Literature by Women*. New York: WW Norton.

Gyekye, Kwame (1978) 'Akan concept of a person', *International Philosophical Quarterly 18*(3): 277–87.

Hagan, George (2010) *'Nyim dze nsaee daze: Cultural affirmation and transvaluation of values'*. First Kobina Sekyi Memorial Lecture, Centre for Advanced Studies of African Society Occasional Paper No. 62. November 1.

Maseko, Zola (1998) *The Life and Times of Sara Baartman – 'Hottentot Venus'*. Brooklyn, New York: First Run/Icarus Films, VHS, 52 minutes.

Morrow, John (1998) *History of Political Thought: A Thematic Introduction*. London: Macmillan Press.

Mumford, Stephen D. (1994) *The Life and Death of NSSM 200: How the Destruction of Political Will Doomed a U.S. Population Policy*. Research Triangle Park, NC: Center for Research on Population and Security.

Muponde, Robert (2013) '"I am well if you are well": Nervous Conditions of Philanthropy in African Culture' in Tade Aina (ed.) *Giving to Help, Helping to Give: The Context and Politics of African Philanthropy*. Dakar: Amalion Publishing/Trust Africa. pp 97–125.

Nakashima, D., Prott, L. and Bridgewater, P. (2000) 'Tapping into the world's wisdom', *UNESCO Sources, 125*, July–August, p. 12.

Nkrumah, Kwame (1963) The African Genius. Speech Delivered at the Formal Opening of the Institute of African Studies, University of Ghana. Accra: Afram Publications.

Olufunmilayo, Arewa (2016) *Cultural Appropriation: When 'Borrowing' Becomes Exploitation, The Conversation*. http://theconversation.com/cultural-appropriation-when-borrowing-becomes-exploitation-57411 (accessed 12 January 2017).

Owolabi, K. (1999) *The Quest for Democracy in Africa: A Theoretical Explanation*. Lagos: O.O.P. Ltd.

Qureshi, Sadiah (2004) 'Displaying Sara Baartman, the "Venus Hottentot"', *History of Science* 42(136): 233–57.

Oyekan, A.O. (2009) 'Democracy and Africa's search for development', *Journal of Pan African Studies* 3(1): 214–26.

Sekyi, Kobina (1997) *The Blinkards, a Comedy; And, The Anglo-Fanti, a Short Story*. African Writers Series, Vol. 136. London: Heinemann.

Strother, Z.S. (1999) 'Display of the Body Hottentot'. In B. Lindfors (ed.), *Africans on Stage: Studies in Ethnological Show Business*. Bloomington, IN: Indiana University Press, pp. 1–55.

Willis, Deborah (2010) *Black Venus 2010: They Called Her 'Hottentot'*. Philadelphia: Temple University Press.

Wingo, Ajume (2008) 'Akan philosophy of the person'. In Edward N. Zalta (ed.), *The Stanford Encyclopedia of Philosophy* (Fall), Stanford, CA.

Wiredu, Kwasi (1992) 'The African concept of personhood'. In Harley E. Flack and Edmund D. Pellegrino (eds), *African-American Perspectives on Biomedical Ethics*. Washington, DC: Georgetown University Press.

6

Pueblos[1] in Movement

Feminist and Indigenous Perspectives from Latin America

Nora Garita Bonilla

The main idea of my exposition: The proposal for the future is in collective action and social movements, and the new sociology is developing in studying these.

1. The expression 'pueblos in movement' is said in the plural, **not in any way do I refer** to the category 'people' as reflected by Ernesto Laclau, which in the singular is essentialist and points to an 'impossible totality' (Laclau 2005: 32).
2. 'Pueblos' is the name given to the indigenous villages or settlements during the period of Spanish colonization in America, and whose existence today is still living presence of colonialism (Quijano, 2012). The term 'pueblos in movement' points to the limits of theories on social movements.
3. Latin America, a unit of reflection? Its colonial past and the pattern of power called 'colonialism' by Quijano after the independence (Quijano, 2012) have established dynamics that allow it to be considered as a unit of reflection.

The question has been raised recurrently throughout the history of the Latin-American sociology, and multiple **typologies** have been made according to the criteria of diverse researchers, especially from very different situations of insertion in the world market.

For the present moment Latin American countries are classified as 'globalized modernization' by Juan Pablo Pérez (2014: 110). His research aims to understand the dynamics of inequalities based on the appropriation of surpluses.

Pérez affirms the existence of 'several Latin Americas':

*   Globalized: represented in areas of major cities where economic globalization activities are performed.

- Opposite end: the Latin America of the 'losers' of the structural adjustment relegated to the extreme social exclusion.
- Between two poles: a Latin America where the State and its national action remain in effect (Pérez, 2014: 112).

This classification serves to contextualize many of today's social movements, and to understand the scales in which they operate: global, local, national, communal.

We Could Say that Latin America is a Unit in Diversity

Heterogeneity of actions, movements, resistance, identity struggles, cannot be explained in full as struggles for the appropriation of surpluses.

Examples: graffiti artists drawing on walls of buildings to prevent 'gentrification' of a neighborhood, collective of the 'diverse kiss' of transgender people, fights of women against obstetric violence. Some of these are closer to what Touraine called 'new social movements' since the 1980s and 1990s, independently of political parties, identity struggles.

Indigenous rebellions in recent decades have not always motivated the dispute over surpluses. Their actions and movements have other identity components **that respond to other logics**. The water war in Bolivia defends water as a common good. The land struggles do not seek individual property but, from its community collective logic, a common territory is defended (Tzul, 2015). Their struggles, such as the ones from women and young people, have been multidimensional. The struggle of Ixil women for the historical memory in the genocide trial in Guatemala, among other epistemologies, from their body-territory violated.

The social theory shows its limits here in interpreting some realities. As it was noted by the intellectual Aymara Juan José Bautista, remembering Marx, 'capitalism created society but destroyed community'. Challenge: develop own categories to understand the particularities of colonialism in its most cultural aspects, beyond the struggles driven by the contradiction of capital/work.

The economic model has led to predatory extractive practices that violate rights of individuals, of communities, of Nature. Even progressive governments have opted for a predator extractivism whose environmental impact is huge, generating a high level of conflict with peasant communities, indigenous and student sectors. In partnership with the media, social protest is criminalized. This is 'extrahection',[2]

while the violatory nature of the rights is intrinsic to the extractivism
(Gudynas, 2016).

In the last congress of the Latin American Association of Sociology
held in Costa Rica, 2015, unpublished work on movements and collective
actions were presented: 'Yo Soy 132 (I am 132)' in Mexico, socio-territorial
conflicts in progressive governments, digital activism, cross-legged movement, social movement of victims, networks against the construction of
dams in Mexico, emergence of social movements in Latin America from
the notion of social networks, the right to the city, or collective actions for
the defense of the territory in Veracruz.

Many presentations at the congress were descriptions lacking theory.
We are facing what Boaventura De Sousa Santos calls 'sub-theorized
practices'. This represents a great challenge to move forward into new
categories and understand the nature of these emancipatory practices.

Critical Thinking and the Social Movements

The tradition of Latin American critical thought drank from the foun-
tains of Marxism, specifically in the Thesis about Feuerbach: 'The philosophers have only interpreted the world in various ways, but now it
is about time to transform it' (Marx, 1845). Meaning, we talk about a
thought emerged from practice and that reverses over it, of reflection
and action linked inseparably.

Sociology as a science emerged in modernity and has been a propi-
tious field for the development of critical thinking. Its future has always
been clashes between a science in the service of hegemony and a science
to build counter-hegemony.

However, the Eurocentric character of critical thinking is what con-
ceived its limits:

1. The first limit: conceive ourselves as universal based on a particular, which
   clashed with this critical thought before each particular. The same reality
   showed how the universal utopias of the Eurocentric thinking clashed with
   the American reality.
2. Paulo Henrique Martins has pointed to the enduring historical tension
   between colonialism and decolonialism, in the same organization of the
   bureaucratic apparatus of the colonial period and in the post-independence,
   the awareness of cultural and historical particularities (Martins, 2012: 26).
3. Mechanical application of thought theories in Europe in the struggles and
   revolutionary movements of the 20th century.

4. Already in the founding moments of sociology as a science in Latin America, in the 60s and 70s of the 20th century, other limits were found in what the theory itself excluded: exclusions from the sociological perspective; critical theory still thinking about an abstract universal subject without ethnicity or body, because women were thought of as an abstract subject 'woman'.

In practice, actions and social movements have always led to critical thinking. Social movements, including especially the feminist, indigenous, and sexual identities' movements, made subjects visible as their thought emerged from specific bodies–territories.

Contributions of Feminisms and Indigenous Resistance to the Social Sciences

The struggles of women for their rights in Europe questioned the abstract universal subject of the Enlightenment. European feminism, however, built another essentialized object – 'woman'. But it is from the edges where the abstract subject is challenged. Afro-Chicano feminism raised the category of 'intersectionality' as an articulation of hierarchies and rationalizations: class, gender, sexualities, race (Lugones, 2008).

Postcolonial feminisms made it clear that the abstract subject 'woman' made invisible the multiplicity of conditions for women. The expression 'third world woman' was an abstraction hiding diversities and had little utility to understand the situation of women (Mohanty, 2008). Meaning, there appeared a gap between theory and place.

In Latin America, Silvia Rivera Cusicanqui (Rivera, 2010) and the Bolivian communitary feminists also reveal the specific complexities of that abstract subject woman. They disclaim the decolonial studies of the United States, given the 'political urgency' of the postcolonial studies in India and the decolonizing feminisms in Latin America.

In Latin America, the urban feminisms of the middle/upper class have struggled for the extension of citizenship to be included in democracy and have made significant struggles against violence and femicide, as in the movement 'Ni una menos (Not one[woman] less)' in Argentina.

There are, however, differences between these feminisms and indigenous feminisms in Latin America. For urban feminists, of the middle and upper class, indigenous feminisms are sexist. For indigenous feminists, the ethnocentrism of feminisms is the reason why it is hard to understand their community approach, which includes men from their community in the struggles against patriarchy and community resistance.

These community feminisms question the separation of human vs. nature, and the Eurocentric logo-centrism. Their starting point for reflection is to be a woman-body pierced by culture, thus opening the way, as did Fanon (1961), to the located thought.

A common point in urban feminisms, community feminisms, eco-feminisms, is exactly that starting-point to express and to think: to be a body-territory – body-territory violated since the conquest of America until today, passing through war violations in Guatemala (Ixil women) or deaths in Ciudad Juárez in Mexico (Segato, 2011) or femicides across the whole continent.

Feminisms have in Latin America been the first to have started what Boaventura de Sousa Santos calls 'sociology of absences and emergencies' (2003, 2006).

Indigenous movements in Latin America, especially in Bolivia and Ecuador, raised from their practices the question about the revolutionary subject.

In their struggle for the defense of the common goods before the interventions of the State or transnational projects backed by the State, the exclusive nature of the nation-state construction was evident. The management of the common goods and struggles for the defense of community logic have proven that neither the State nor the market are the only administrators of the common goods, as noted by Elinor Ostrom (Poteete et al., 2012: 107).

These movements were able to incorporate within the constitutions of Bolivia and Ecuador the existence of many nations under a single state. The contribution of these indigenous people was in interrogating the State/ Nation relationship.

Their contributions have gone much further, by questioning the linearity of the conceptions of development and stopping development jargons. And they propose from their worldviews the 'Pacha Mama' as an alternative to development itself is not synonymous with the Western concept of Nature but 'a way to be understood as part of a social community and ecologically extended' (Gudynas, 2015: 143). In this sense, their proposals can be called 'post-development': a deconstruction of the idea of development.

A common point of alliance between the indigenous movements, peasant movements and the full range of Latin American eco-feminisms against the extractivism, are their proposals around the ancient 'good life' or 'living well', that does not intend a return to previous centuries, but to other *alternative modernities*.

The Zapatista movement is building proposals in the present that illuminate visions of the future. We can mention some:

- A new conception of democracy: mandar obediciendo (to lead by obeying).
- A subversion of gender hierarchies, having women commanders and men deputy-commanders.
- Their struggle is not cultural conservatism itself, but a bet on the rationality of life.

Indigenous communities are not state-centric. Their 'snails' are building spaces of management of 'the communes'. The Zapatismo does not seek indigenous essentialisms, but foreshadows an alternative modernity (Millán, 2011).

Imagine the Future Along with the Pueblos in Movement

The wealth of 'sub-theorized' actions, movements and resistances opens a field for generating new categories. It is a favorable environment to the renewal of theoretical approaches.

To the long tradition of critical Latin American thought, today categories and concepts are added that have been built within Latin American critical thinking along with the social movements. I mention the category 'extractivism' and other concepts – 'body-territory', 'patriarchal entronque' (roughly, partriachal relationship), colonialism of gender, 'extrahection', good living, and the rights of Nature.

We cannot imagine the future from fantasies, but we can conceive it with the seeds of future planted by collective actions and social movements.

For the indigenous Maya and Inca, time does not pass linearly, but with a circular motion. The quechua term *ñawpa pacha* designates the past time and means time–space ahead (Laurencich-Minelli, 2000). That is why in many representations in drawings or carved stones, the past is drawn or represented in front of the characters. Meaning, the future is behind. This means, in solidarity spaces around the common goods we find the harbinger of the future.

The struggles for common goods – water, community territory, right to a life without violence towards women, which are the sparks of the future built from social movements – are in an intersection or point of convergence with other struggles of global scale: free access to intellectual production, the right to move around the city without violence.

The assertion of Pierre Salama (2015) is certain, that we live in a world where we cannot ignore the 'commons', but also that the commercial is dominant.

The warning does not diminish the fact that there is, from the struggle for common goods, a point of **convergence in the struggles**. Hence, the theory of the common as 'the political principle from which we must build commons … it is the political principle that defines a new regime of struggles worldwide' (Dardot and Laval, 2015: 49).

Ties intersect to form a fabric – this is the new proposal of pluriversal struggle that signifies the start of a change in civilization.

Notes

1   Pueblos can be translated in English as peoples or communities. The word pueblos is retained here to avoid either of these two narrower English terms.

2   'Extrahection' (*extrahección*) is a term proposed to describe extractive industries that rip out the earth's natural resources in violation of human rights and those of nature; the definition appears at: http://ambiental.net/wp-content/uploads/2015/12/Gudynas ApropiacionExtractivismoExtraheccionesOdeD2013.pdf.

References and Further Readings

Aguinaga, M., et al. (2012) *Pensar desde el feminismo: críticas y alternativas al desarrollo, Más allá del desarrollo*. Mexico: Ediciones Fundación Rosa Luxemburgo.

Bidaseca, K. and Vázquez, L. (2011) *Feminismos y poscolonialidad*. Buenos Aires: Ediciones Godot.

Bruckmann, M. and Dos Santos, T. (2008) Soziale Bewegungen in Lateinamerika Eine historische Bilanz. Revue PROKLA número 142. www.prokla.de/wp/wp-content/uploads/2006/Prokla142.pdf (accessed April 2018).

Dessalines, 1805, Constitución imperial de Haití. Consultado en: https://decolonialucr.files.wordpress.com/2014/09/constitucion-imperial-de-haiti-1805-bilbioteca-ayacucho.pdf.

Dardot, P. and Laval, C. (2015) *Commun: Essai sur la révolution au XXIe siècle*. Paris: La Découverte.

de Sousa Santos, B. (2003) *La caída del Angelus Novus: ensayos para una nueva teoría social y una nueva práctica política*. Bogotá: Ediciones Antropos.

de Sousa Santos, B. (2006) Capítulo I: La Sociología de las Ausencias y la Sociología de las Emergencias: para una ecología de saberes. *Renovar la teoría crítica y reinventar la emancipación social (encuentros en Buenos Aires)*. ISBN 987-1183-57-7. http://bibliotecavirtual.clacso.org.ar/ar/libros/edicion/santos/Capitulo%20I.pdf (accessed April 2018).

Fanon, F. (1961) *Los condenados de la tierra*. www.matxingunea.org/media/pdf/Fanon_
Los_condenados_de_la_tierra_def_web_2.pdf (accessed 16 April 2013).

Fernández, V. (2011) *Consideraciones sobre los feminismos en América Latina,
Feminismos y poscolonialidad*. Buenos Aires: Ediciones Godot.

Gudynas, E. (2012) *Debates sobre el desarrollo y sus alternativas en América latina: una
breve guía heterodoxa, Más allá del desarrollo*. Mexico: Ediciones Fundación Rosa
Luxemburgo.

Gudynas, E. (2015) *Derechos de la Naturaleza. Etica biocéntrica y políticas ambientales*.
Buenos Aires: Tinta Limón.

Gudynas, E. (2016) Taller impartido en el congreso pre-ALAS en la Universidad de Villa
María, Córdoba, Argentina, June 2016.

Hinkelammert, F. (2015) El vaciamiento de los derechos humanos en la estrategia de la
globalización, conferencia impartida en el congreso ALAS-2015 Costa Rica. Available
at sociología-alas.org.

Hinkelammert, F. (1984) *Crítica a la razón utópica*. Costa Rica: DEI.

Laclau, E. (2005) *La razón populista*. Mexico: FCE.

Laurencich-Minelli, L. (2000) *The Inca World*. Norman, OK: University of Oklahoma
Press.

Lugones, M. (2005) 'Multiculturalismo radical y feminismos de mujeres de color', *Revista
Internacional de Filosofía Política 25*: 61–75.

Lugones, M. (2008) Colonialidad y género: Hacia un feminismo descolonial. In
W Mignolo, *Género y descolonialidad*. Buenos Aires: Ediciones del signo.

Martins, P. (2012) *La decolonialidad de América Latina y la heterotopía de una comunidad de destino solidaria*. Argentina: Ediciones CICCUS.

Marx, K. (1845) Tesis sobre Feuerbach. Retrieved from www.ehu.eus/Jarriola/Docencia/
EcoMarx/TESIS%20SOBRE%20FEUERBACH%20Thesen%20ueber%20Feuerbach.
pdf (accessed April 2018).

Millán, M. (2011) Feminismos, poscolonialidad, descolonización: ¿del centro a los márgenes?
www.scielo.org.mx/scielo.php?script=sci_arttext&pid=S1870-00632011000300002
(accessed April 2018).

Mohanty, C. (2008) Bajo los ojos de Occidente: academia feminista y discursos colonials.
In L. Suárez Navaz and R. Hernández (eds), *Descolonizando el feminismo. Teorías y
prácticas desde los márgenes*. Madrid: Cátedra.

Molina, J. and Grosser, V. (2008) La construcción del 'pueblo', según Laclau. *La Lámpara
de Diógenes*, *9*(16–17): 137–57.

Ostrom, E. (2011) *El gobierno de los bienes comunes. La evolución de las instituciones de
acción colectiva*. Mexico: FCE.

Pérez Saínz, J.P. (2014) *Mercados y bárbaros. La persistencia de las desigualdades de
excedente en América Latina*. Costa Rica: FLACSO.

Poteete, A.R., Janslen, M.A. and Ostrom E. (2012) *Trabajar juntos. Acción colectiva-
bienes comunes y múltiples métodos en la práctica*. Mexico: FCE.

Quijana, A. (2012) 'Buen vivir': entre el "desarrollo" y la des coloniolidad del poder',
Revista Viento Sur, 122: 45–56.

Rivera Cusicanqui, S. (2010) *Ch'ixinakax utxiwa: una reflexión sobre prácticas y discursos descolonizadores*. Buenos Aires: Tinta Limón.

Salama, P. (2015) Argentina, Brasil, México entran en la tormenta. ¿Quo vadis América Latina? *Revista Herramienta*, Web 17 July, Buenos Aires.

Segato, R.L. (2011) Femigenocidio y feminicidio: una propuesta de tipificación. Leído en la mesa 'Feminismos Poscoloniales y descoloniales: otras epistemologías' durante el II Encuentro Mesoamericano de Estudios de Género y Feminismos, 4–6 May 2011, Ciudad de Guatemala. Retrieved from www.herramienta.com.ar/autores/segato-rita-laura.

Segato, R.L. (2013) *La escritura en el cuerpo de las mujeres asesinadas en Ciudad Juárez*. Buenos Aires: Tinta Limón.

Spivak, G.C. (2010) ¿Puede hablar el subalterno?, Cuadernos de Plata, Buenos Aires.

Svampa, M. and Viale, E. (2015) *Maldesarrollo. La Argentina del extractivismo y el despojo*. Buenos Aires: Altuna ediciones.

Tilly, C. (1978) *From Mobilization to Revolution*. Reading, MA: Addison-Wesley.

Tilly, C. and Tarrow, S. (2006) *Contentious Politics*. Boulder, CO: Paradigm Publishers.

Torres Rivas, E. (2011) *Revoluciones sin cambios revolucionarios*. Guatemala: F y G editores.

Touraine, A. (1977) *The Self-reproduction of Society*. Chicago: University of Chicago Press.

Touraine, A. (1988) *Return of the Actor: Social Theory in Postindustrial Society*. Minnesota: University of Minnesota Press.

Touraine, A. (1989) *América Latina: política y sociedad*. Madrid: Espasa Calpe.

Tzul, G. (2015) Conferencia en el XXX congreso latinoamericanos de sociología, ALAS, Costa Rica. http://sociologia-alas.org/congreso-xxx/conferencias/.

Vazquez, V. (2008) Las contribuciones del feminismo poscolonial a los estudios de género: interseccionalidad, racismo y mujeres subalternas. http://www.perfiles.cult.cu/article.php?article_id=267.

Zaffaroni, E. (2011) *La Pachamama y el humano*. Buenos Aires: Ediciones Madres de la Plaza de Mayo.

7

Post-Islamist Democracy

Asef Bayat

In May 2016, the congress of the Tunisian Islamic party al-Nahda convened to move overwhelmingly to 'completely separate religious activities from political activities'. Al-Nahda's leader Rachid Ghannouchi confirmed that "we are no longer an Islamist party, but a party of Muslim Democrats".[1] Can there be such a thing as 'Muslim Democracy'? And if so, what is it and how different may it be from liberal democracy? It might sound far-fetched to pose such a question at a global time when liberal democracy is challenged by the onslaught of rightist populism spreading from India to Europe and the United States, the time when neoliberal globalization, inequality, exclusion, and everyday anxiety have bolstered support for nativism and authoritarian polity. The idea of Muslim democracy may sound even more suspect when the pornographic images of al-Qaeda's violence and ISIS brutalities in the international media generate serious doubt about the confluence of Islam with democratic values and institutions. The descent of Recep Tayyip Erdoğan's Turkey into an authoritarian polity seems to render even the notions of 'moderate' or 'liberal Islam' overly uncertain.

Yet if sociology is serious about envisioning alternative futures, if it possesses adequate methodological tools and analytical insights to reflect not merely on the past and the present but also on possibilities for change, we should then be able to place such ideas as 'Muslim democracy' under sober and serious scrutiny.[2] This chapter considers Islam as a site of intense struggle by competing Muslim groups to give different meanings to their faith, including authoritarian as well as democratic. It argues that while 'Islamism' as a political project building on people's 'obligations' espouses hostility towards democratic governance, post-Islamism can and does embrace democratic polity because it recognizes people's rights. In this sense it should be plausible to imagine a post-Islamic democracy wherein secular governance may cohabit, albeit in tension, with the active presence of religion in the public sphere.

Debate

In the past two decades or so there has been a heated debate about the compatibility of Islam and democracy – and by extension modernity; about whether or not there can be a possibility of what Rachid Ghannouchi perceives as Muslim democracy, but I have called post-Islamist democracy. Given the recent political conditions in the world – the rise of Islamist governments, violence of al-Qaeda, and more recently the establishment by ISIS of an 'Islamic caliphate' in Iraq and Syria – the answer has often been in the negative. The critiques often focus on the experiences of Islamist Iran, Pakistan or the Jihadi movements to demonstrate the inherent anti-democratic spirit of Islam. Others refer to certain key 'principles' in Islam to suggest that this religion cannot by its very nature embrace democratic ethos.[3] For instance, in Islam, they say, sovereignty belongs to God, not people; as a result the model of governance in Islam remains inherently theocratic, and not democratic. In addition, Islam's position on women demonstrates its 'misogyny' and rejection of equality, and its 'violent' precepts establishes intolerance and exclusivist polity in which dialogue finds little place. Beyond these prevalent suggestions, spread largely in the mainstream media outlets, a number of serious scholars also express doubt about the possibility of imagining some kind of 'post-Islamist democracy'. In the final plenary session of the International Sociological Association in Vienna, July 2016, the prominent French sociologist Alain Touraine offered a categorical 'no' to the question – 'can we imagine a Muslim democracy'. 'Muslim democracy is as impossible as a Christian or Jewish democracy', Touraine proclaimed; because, 'God's law is by nature eternal; whereas men's laws are by nature historical: what a majority has decided another one can cancel it,' he argued. According to Touraine, 'the basic condition for democracy is laïcity, that is the separation of political power from religious authority.'

Touraine spoke of 'God's law' as if he truly believed that God had indeed spoken his 'eternal law' to humanity, overlooking the fact that

'God's laws' are materialized only through the often-contested interpretations of certain humans – clerics, theocrats, or others – who may claim to rule in the name of enforcing 'God's eternal laws' (as powerful men did the European medieval Church); but today many Christians do not find any necessary conflicts between their faith and democratic polity. Given the experience of 'Christian democracy' in Europe or Latin America, it is curious why Touraine considers an idea of Christian democracy simply 'impossible'.[4] What is still more probing is that even if the idea of Christian democracy is considered legitimate, the idea of 'Muslim democracy' is for the most part considered dubious, even if Muslim democrats adhere to the separation of 'political power from religious authority'. This partly reflects the familiar Orientalist exceptionalism that has hovered around the analyses of Islam and Muslims for long. Instead of proclaiming 'impossible', one should legitimately ask what is meant by 'Christian Democracy' or Muslim Democracy.

Here, I do not wish to delve into philosophical discussions or draw on Islamic 'tenets' and texts to examine if Islam can embrace democratic ethos. Rather, as a sociologist, I like to focus on the actual experience, on Muslims' multiple and conflictive deployments of the 'tenets' and texts. I wish to focus not on faith, but the faithful; not Islam as a doctrine, but Muslims as the embodiments of the doctrine. For as I have argued elsewhere, the question of compatibility of Islam and democracy is not as much philosophical as it is political. It is primarily a matter of political struggle to define the core values of Islam.[5] Accordingly, it becomes evident that there is neither an inherent contradiction nor a necessary convergence between 'Islam' (which Islam?) and democracy (what type?). This may be true not just with respect to Islam, but also with other religious traditions. In real life Islam remains a site of intense struggle between different groups and individuals who ultimately define its spirit. Some deploy it as an ethical frame for personal salvation, some turn it into an ideology to rule, a structure for tyranny; while others render it as an ideology for revolution, and still others attempt to make it work with democratic polity. I have proposed that Islamism and post-Islamism may represent two different trajectories through which one can spell out the relationship between Islam and democratic governance. Islamism represents broadly an undemocratic and exclusivist polity, whereas post-Islamism may offer a possible model of inclusive post-Islamist democracy.

Islamism

By Islamism, I mean those ideologies and movements that want to establish some kind of an Islamic order – a religious state, sharia law, and
moral codes in the Muslim societies and communities. Association with
the state is a key feature of the Islamist movements. Islamist movements
are adamant to control the state power not only because it ensures their
rule, but especially because they consider the state as the most powerful and efficient institution through which they are able, through *da'wa*
(preaching) or duress, to enforce the Quaranic dictum of 'Command Good
and Forbid Wrong', to spread 'good' and eradicate 'evil' in Muslim societies. This means that the Islamists' normative and legal perspectives
place more emphasis on people's obligations than their rights; people are
perceived more as dutiful subjects than rightful citizens. In this sense,
Islamism is basically a duty-centered religious polity. The mode of governance adopted by Iran's hardliners, Pakistani Jama't-i Islami or Lashkar
Tayyuba, the Indonesian Lashkar Jihad, the Somali Shabab al-Islami,
or Egypt's Muslim Brotherhood exemplify this type of exclusivist and
undemocratic polity.

But Islamist movements vary in terms of different ways in which they
are to achieve their strategic goals. The *reformist* trends aspire ultimately
to establish an Islamic state, but wish to do so gradually, peacefully, and
within the existing constitutional frameworks which they hope to alter.
These include the 'electoral Islamists' such as the Muslim Brotherhood in
the Arab countries, the Jama'at-i Islami in Pakistan, or Jama's al-Islamiyya
after the Egyptian revolution of 2011.The *revolutionary* or *militant* trends
such as the pre-revolution Jama'a al-Islamiya in Egypt, the Algerian FIS,
Lashkar Jihad in Indonesia, or Hizbual-Tahrir and Lashkar al-Tayyiba in
Pakistan resort to violence and terrorism against state agencies, Western
targets and non-Muslim civilians, hoping to cause a Leninist-type insur-
rection to seize state power which would then unleash Islamization of
social order from above. The Jihadi trends such as the groups associated
with al-Qaeda are somewhat different. While militant Islamism represents
political movements operating within the given nation-states and targeting the national states, most Jihadis are transnational in their ideas and
operations and often represent apocalyptic 'ethical movements' involved
in 'civilizational struggles' with the aim of combating such highly abstract
targets as the 'corrupt West' or societies of 'non-believers'. For many
Jihadis the very struggle itself, or jihad, becomes an end in itself. Olivier

Roy goes so far as arguing that groups associated with the ISIS pursue not simply Islam; rather they embrace nihilism and death; their preoccupation is not da'wa to spread Islam in society and polity, but to frame their radicalization in terms of radical Islam.[6]

Post-Islamism

In 1995, I wrote an essay entitled the 'Coming of a Post-Islamist Society' in which I discussed the articulation of the remarkable social trends, political perspectives, and religious thought which post-Khomeini Iran had begun to witness – a trend which eventually came to embody the 'reform movement' of the late 1990s.[7] My tentative essay dealt only with the societal trends for there was little at the governmental level that I could consider 'post-Islamist'. Indeed, as originally used, post-Islamism pertained only to the realities of the Islamic Republic of Iran, and not to other settings and societies. Yet the core spirit of the term referred to the metamorphosis of Islamism (in ideas, approaches, and practices) from within and without.

Since then, a number of observers in Europe and beyond have deployed the term, even though often descriptively, to refer primarily to what they consider a general shift in attitudes and strategies of Islamist militants in the Muslim world. In these early usages 'post-Islamism' was deployed primarily as a temporal rather than analytical category representing a 'particular era' or the 'end of a historical phase'.[8] Yet the term 'post-Islamism' and the perspective it projects has thus far prompted a widespread debate and sizeable literature both in the West as well as the Muslim majority countries notably Indonesia, Malaysia, Iran, Turkey and the Arab countries, notably Tunisia.[9]

In my formulation, post-Islamism represented both a *condition* and a *project*. In the first instance, post-Islamism referred to a political and social condition where, following a phase of experimentation, the appeal, energy, and sources of legitimacy of Islamism gets exhausted even among its once-ardent supporters. Islamists become aware of their discourse's anomalies and inadequacies as they attempt to institutionalize or imagine their rule. The continuous trial and error, pushed by global forces and national realities, would make the framework susceptible to questions and criticisms. Eventually, pragmatic attempts to maintain the system reinforce abandoning certain of its underlying principles. Islamism becomes compelled, both by its own internal contradictions and by societal pressure, to reinvent itself, but does so at the cost of a qualitative shift.

The tremendous transformation in religious and political discourse in Iran during the 1990s or in Turkey in 2000s exemplified this tendency.

Not only a condition, post-Islamism is also as a project, a conscious attempt to conceptualize and strategize the rationale and modalities of transcending Islamism in social, political, and intellectual domains. In this sense it denotes a critique of Islamism from within and without. Yet post-Islamism is neither anti-Islamic nor un-Islamic or secular. Rather it represents an endeavor to fuse religiosity and rights, faith and freedom, Islam and liberty. It is an attempt to turn the underlying principles of Islamism on its head by emphasizing rights instead of mere duties, plurality in place of singular authoritative voice, historicity rather than fixed scriptures, and the future instead of the past. It wants to marry Islam with democracy and modernity, to achieve what some have termed as an 'alternative modernity'. Thus, whereas Islamism is defined by the fusion of religion and responsibility, post-Islamism emphasizes religiosity and rights. It favors a civil non-religious state, but accords an active role for religion in the public sphere. It thus simultaneously advocates a secular (non-religious) state but a pious society. A number of experiments have come to reflect this post-Islamist polity in the Muslim majority countries including Iran's reformist government under President Mohamed Khatami (1997–2004), the Justice and Development Party (AKP) in Turkey before its leader Recep Tayyip Erdoğan retreated to an authoritarian path, the Justice and Development Party (PJD) in Morocco, the Prosperous Justice Party in Indonesia, and al-Nahda under Rachid Ghannouchi in Tunisia. These trends exemplify varying degrees of post-Islamism in the past two decades or so. These political trends, like Christian Democracy, may be socially or morally conservative; but they are not necessarily Islamist.

Diverse Trajectories

Most of these post-Islamist trends evolved from a more or less Islamist past, but the trajectories and reasons for change in each of these trends have been quite different. In Iran for instance, the end of the war with Iraq (1988), the death of Ayatollah Khomeini (1989), and the program of post-war reconstruction under President Rafsanjani marked the onset of what I called 'post-Islamism'. As a master movement, Iran's post-Islamism was embodied in remarkable social and intellectual trends and movements, expressed in religiously innovative discourses by youths, students, women, and religious intellectuals, who demanded democracy, individual rights, tolerance, and gender equality as well as the separation of religious authority from political power. Yet they refused to throw away religious sensibilities altogether. The daily resistance and struggles of ordinary actors compelled religious thinkers, spiritual elites, and political actors to undertake a crucial paradigmatic shift. Scores of old Islamist revolutionaries renounced their earlier ideas, lamenting the danger of the religious state to both religion and the state. In a sense, the Islamic state in Iran generated adversaries from both without and within, who called for the secularization of the state, but stressed maintaining religious ethics in society.

The AKP in Turkey evolved from the Islamist experience of Melli Gorush, which since the 1970s went through different incarnations and re-inventions in its battle with the intransigent Kemalist secular ideas and institutions. The transformation took place because the early Islamists were compelled to respond to the secular sensibilities of the military, vocal citizens, and the exigencies of joining the European Union. They pushed for a secular state, not the type hostile to religion (as in French laicity), but rather a neutral state (as in the United States) where religion and religiosity could thrive.[10] This rather self-serving adoption of secular state inevitably moved Turkey away from embracing the model of Islamic state practiced in Iran or elsewhere.

The trajectory of PJD in Morocco is somewhat different. It originated from the Shebab Islamiyya, an Islamist group in the college, which King Hasan had encouraged in the 1970s to grow against leftist ideas and movements. But as is often the case, the Islamist Shebab grew beyond its permitted mandate, instigating the regime surveillance and suppression, forcing its leadership into exile. The suppression and exile pushed the leaders to re-evaluate and rethink their Islamist project, leading in the long run to the creation of the gradualist and legalist PJD under Benkirani who served as the Prime Minister of Morocco between 2011 and 2017.

In Indonesia after the fall of Suharto dictatorship militant Islamism thrived under democracy, alarming many Muslim activists and thinkers about what they saw as the great injury Islamist radicalism had inflicted on Indonesian Islam, society and its newly born democracy. They were compelled to come forward to redress the situation by offering a different post-Islamist agenda. Outspoken groups such as the Liberal Islamic Network, the Wahid Institute, and Ma'arif Institute for Culture and Harmony took up the banner of a critical campaign to present 'true' Islam as opposed to that of the militants. But the most important trend currently is the Prosperous Justice Party (PKS). The PKS originated from an Islamist past but later changed course and began to work within the democratic system of Indonesia, and has increased its votes as a result.

In Egypt, the change has been more complex. The Muslim Brotherhood, the most organized and powerful Islamist movement in the world, with estimated 3 million members, had begun to undergo some discursive changes in the 2000s by speaking pragmatically of democracy, elections, minority rights, women's rights. But this shift in discourse was pushed largely by events – notably the Bush administration's dialogue with the Brotherhood and emphasis on democracy – rather than resulting from a systematic evaluation of their Islamist and exclusive ideology. Earlier, a faction with a somewhat post-Islamist orientation had broken away from the Muslim Brothers to form its own independent entity as Hizb al-Wasat. But crucial shake-ups came after the Egyptian revolution of 2011. The conflicting statements of different Brotherhood leaders in post-Mubarak Egypt pointed to a growing discord within the group. The old guard continued to speak of Islamism and shari'a, with leaders such as Mohammed Badi' and Mahmoud Ezzat remaining committed to the ideas of Sayyid Qutb on issues of internal discipline and organization. But the revolutionary events and the brief rule of the Brothers profoundly unsettled the movement, causing splits, expulsions, and erosion. The popular Abdel-Monem Abul-Fotuh was expelled, who then formed his own Party of Strong Egypt. Along with dozens of prominent members, many youths of the Brotherhood embraced post-Islamism of AKP type, lashing out on their old-guard leadership for its authoritarianism, secrecy, and gender bias. In an early wave of defections, the youths of Muslim Brothers formed five new political parties, including Tayyar Misry and Hizb al-Adl, all standing in opposition to the Brotherhood's leadership. More importantly, the two short years of the Brothers' regime cost the group an unprecedented loss in sympathy and support among ordinary Egyptians. The ascendency of General Sisi to power and the suppression of the Brotherhood since 2013 has already caused further splits in strategy and ideology within the movement.

None of these experiences would match the 'post-Islamist' articulation of the Tunisian al-Nahda party led by Rachid Ghanoushi. Winning the largest votes in elections for the Constituent Assembly and Parliament after the 2011 Revolution, al-Nahda emphatically remained committed to a secular democratic state, separation of religious authority from political power, but wished to promote a pious society. Even though the secular forces remained suspicious of its inner intents, al-Nahda went on to help pass the most democratic constitution in the Arab world. In a major doc-trinal shift in May 2016, al-Nahda announced a complete separation of religious from political affairs, moving 'beyond its origin as an Islamist party and has fully embraced a new identity as a party of Muslim demo-crats', proclaimed the leader Ghannouchi in a *Foreign Affairs* article.[11] He argued that under democracy there is no need for a movement to base its politics on defending religion; rather the aim should be to safeguard the inclusive and democratic governance. In the words of Ghannouchi, '[al-Nahda's] evolution should serve as evidence that Islam is indeed compatible with democracy and that Islamic movements can play a vital, constructive role in fostering successful democratic transitions'.[12]

Related to the ideological shake-ups among the Islamist movements has been a change in societal sensibilities. A value survey conducted between June–August 2011 (in Egypt, Iraq, Lebanon, and Saudi Arabia) confirmed that the revolutions were indeed post-Islamist and mostly post-ideological. In Egypt, for instance, some 85% of respondents had stated that the revolution was for democracy, economic prosperity, and equal-ity, while only 9% claimed it to be for Islamic government. This result was confirmed by a TNS poll on Egypt suggesting that 75% of Egyptians wanted a civil, rather than religious state.

Clearly the forms, depth, and spread of post-Islamist experiences have in practice varied. Yet, they all point to some varied shift in vision. In each of these cases, post-Islamism denotes a critical discursive departure or pragmatic exit from an Islamist ideological package characterized broadly by the monopoly of religious truth, exclusivism, and emphasis on obliga-tions, towards acknowledging pluralism, inclusion, flexibility, and more emphasis on rights.

Retreat?

Since the outbreak of the Arab uprisings, a number of political devel-opments have led some to express doubt about the viability of the post-Islamist project. For over a decade the AKP's 'Turkish model' captured the imagination of many observers as an effective instance of 'Muslim democracy' before it descended into the aggressive authoritarianism of the AKP leader Tayyib Erdoğan. Earlier, the AKP pushed Turkey towards a multi-party democracy and economic growth; it undermined the control of the Kemalist 'deep state', struck a deal with the Kurdish opposition, abolished the death penalty, and prepared to join the European Union.

The 'Turkish model', a mix of Islamic piety, electoral democracy, and neoliberal economy, became a dream of many Muslim democrats in the world. As early as 1994, Erdoğan as the Islamic Mayor of Istanbul had become an avid advocate of the book *Who Needs an Islamic State?*, in which the Sudanese Muslim intellectual Abdelwahab el-Effendi relinquishes a 'non-viable' idea of an Islamic state in favour of democracy. Even on his 2011 visit to Cairo just after the Egyptian revolution, Erdoğan called on the Muslim Brothers to discard the idea of Islamic state and adopt secular democracy. However, in the past few years, he began to exhibit an unmistakably autocratic posture, intolerance, and suppression of dissent – rounding up thousands of opposition activists, journalists, teachers, professors, NGOs, and Kurdish parliamentarians in particular after the 2016 coup attempt, opening the way for his plan to turn Turkey into a presidential system in which he could consolidate his autocratic rule.

But what do all these have to do with Islam and Islamism? Do they mean that Erdoğan and his AKP have reverted to Islamism? Indeed it is a question about what role Islam has, if any at all, in these processes. Thus far there is little evidence that the AKP has invoked the Islamization of the state, or deployed Islam as a legitimizing ideology to push for autocracy. If anything, insistence on AKP's 'Islamist refashioning' has obscured a sound analysis to uncover the real causes behind Erdoğan's drive towards authoritarian polity.[13] Did the regional strife, the Syrian civil war and the role of the Kurds in it, the EU's denial of Turkish membership, or unchallenged electoral victories not play a part in his journey? Or perhaps we need different explanations, given that nationalist authoritarianism has become a hallmark of our current global politics, with demagogic autocrats emerging in Russia, India, Philippines, as well as Europe and Donald Trump's America.

Whatever one's reading may be about the relapse of the 'Turkish model', still all attention has focused on the state, with little examination of post-Islamist sensibilities in society, the popular support base for such a polity. The fact is that the retreat of post-Islamist governance (as in Iran after president Muhamad Khatami, or Turkish AKP after the Gezi episode) does not necessarily mean the end of the post-Islamist experience altogether. The idea can survive and even prosper to bring post-Islamist governments to power. In Iran, for instance, the post-Islamist sensibilities continued to persist even after the reformist President Khatami government was replaced by the hardline Islamist Ahmadinejad; in fact it grew to form a mass support for the candidacy of Mir Hussein Mousawi in the presidential elections of 2008, in which the claim of fraud was galvanized in a powerful Green Movement that posed the greatest challenge to the Islamist establishment.[14]

The Turkish experience might have little do with Islamism, but how to speak of post-Islamist inclusion and tolerance at a time when a group like ISIS takes over cities in Iraq and Syria, declares an Islamic caliphate, imposes brutal moral codes, burns alive 'wrong-doers', and terrorizes Muslims and non-Muslims alike for non-compliance? Has the mere emergence of ISIS not questioned the viability of post-Islamism? As I have suggested, the rise of post-Islamism does not mean the end of Islamist polity, nor does it mean the demise of violence perpetrated in the name of Islamist rule. But the key question is how much popular support the movements like ISIS would enjoy. In reality, ISIS received extremely little sympathy among ordinary Muslims, ranging from 0.4% in Jordan to 6.4% in Palestine, according to the Arab Barometer survey.[15] If anything, the brutality of ISIS and its stern opposition to Muslim cultures pushed many ordinary citizens away from the very idea of a religious state. The initial success of ISIS in capturing territories in Iraq had a great deal to do with the discontent among many Iraqi Sunnis caused by the American invasion and the sectarianism of Shi'ite rule in Iraq, which offered an opportunity for the embattled Ba'thist army personnel to take revenge by closing ranks with the Jihadi groups in Iraq and Syria. Yet once ISIS established its brutal rule in its capital Raqqa, Muslim subjects only looked for a chance to flee the caliphate – some 60% of Raqqa's one million population left the city after the arrival of ISIS in 2013, despite heavy-handed restrictions on emigration including confiscation of property.[16]

Surely the authoritarian retreat in AKP and the rise of ISIS have posed a challenge to democratic experience in Turkey and its prospect in Iraq. But none has essentially questioned the viability of post-Islamism as a project and the feasibility of democracy in Muslim majority societies.

Post-Islamist Democracy?

Let me make it clear that I am speaking of post-Islamism, not 'post-Islam' as a temporal signifier. Post-Islamism does not mean exiting from Islam; it means existing from Islamism. Post-Islamism remains religious, but upholds a different, more inclusive, perception about religious polity. Yet it is one in which Islam nevertheless continues to remain important both as a personal faith and as a player in the public sphere. Therefore, it is not correct to claim, as some have, that this new type of religious polity (post-Islamism) differs only in form and is simply a variant of the broad Islamist paradigm. The fact is, the AKP represented a qualitative departure from Melli Gorus, as did the Iranian 'reformists' like Mir-Hussain Mousavi from the Islamists such as Ayatollah Ali Khamenei; with the same token, the post-Islamism of the Sudanese Mahmoud Taha differed in significant ways from the exclusivist Islamism of the Mahdi movement.

We should also be cautious not to confuse the 'electoral Islamism' with 'post-Islamism'. 'Electoral Islamism' refers to the reformist Islamist movements (such as the Muslim Brotherhood, the current Gama'a al-Islamiya in Egypt, or Jama'at-e Islami in Pakistan) which instead of resorting to violence and revolution, join the electoral structure, follow legal procedures, and remain part of the system, to pursue a gradualist strategy of Islamizing the society and the state. Of course, working within the system, so to speak, may (or may not) change them, but until then, they remain Islamist. Despite working within the electoral structure of Pakistan, the Jama'at Islami has not shifted substantially in its strategic vision on religious polity, even though it has given rise to a number of spin-offs.[17]

Are we not then speaking of 'liberal Islam' or 'Islamic liberalism'? If 'liberal Islam' means an interpretation of Islam that accommodates modern democracy, a civil non-religious state, freedom of thought, and human progress, then certainly this shares considerably with post-Islamist thought. But 'post-Islamism' is more than just what it projects, it is also about what it transcends. It is, in other words, a critique of something else. If, on the other hand, 'liberal Islam' implies 'privatization' of Islam, then this is not what the post-Islamists advocate. Because post-Islamists still want religion to be present in the public arena, and wish to promote piety in society. And if 'liberal Islam' is taken to mean an Islam that respects individual rights and freedoms, then we need to consider the relationship between the post-Islamist polity and liberalism. And it is here that one of the key challenges of post-Islamism lies. I think that the post-Islamist project is yet to determine how much individual freedom is compatible with the public piety that it so passionately promotes. So far only Iran under the reformists (1997–2004), Turkey under the AKP, and Tunisia under the Islamic al-Nahda party have experienced some forms of post-Islamist rule. And the result is a mixed bag, in which al-Nahda has proven to be more 'liberal' than others. Some degree of clash may be inevitable. Yet the likely clash between post-Islamist sensibilities and liberal values might (depending on the extent of clash) settle in some kind of 'less-liberal' or 'illiberal' democracy, where electoral democracy may go along with some variable restrictions on liberties, such as restrictions on gender demands, intellectual or artistic productions, or on a desire for alternative life-styles.

Such tensions are not restricted to post-Islamist polity. Historically, Western democracies have also experienced at most parts in their development certain restrictions on individual and civil liberties, as in gay marriage, gender equality, and civil rights. However, if electoral democracy even in its less-liberal form persists, it can open the space for debate over, and possibly extend the scope of these very liberties. But this will depend on painstaking and persistent efforts of democrats to extend the depth and scope of their democracy. However, in the current Muslim majority societies, this project may not succeed without incorporating the principle of social justice and equity—a principle deeply missing from the current actually-existing democracies, weather liberal, illiberal or post-Islamist, for they have all taken, in varied degrees, neoliberal rationality for granted. If post-Islamist democracy is to have a viable future it has to take seriously social justice into its corpse, turning itself into post-Islamist social democracy.

Notes and References

1 Rachid Ghannouchi, 'From Political Islam to Muslim Democracy: The Ennahda Party and the Future of Tunisia', Foreign Affairs, September/October 2016; https://www. foreignaffairs.com/articles/tunisia/political-islam-muslim-democracy.

2 Markus S. Schulz, 'Debating Futures: Global Trends, Alternative Visions, and Public Discourse', *International Sociology*, vol. 31, no. 1 (2016).

3 For instance, see Bernard Lewis, "The Roots of Muslim Rage", *Foreign Policy*, vol. 17, no.4, Summer 2001/2002; and https://www.huffingtonpost.com/alon-benmeir/is-islam-compatible-with_b_3562579.html.

4 Alain Touraine's comments to papers turned out to be too long so that there remained, regrettably, no time for the panelists, including myself, to raise such questions.

5 See Asef Bayat, *Making Islam Democratic* (Stanford University Press, Stanford, CA, 2007).

6 Olivier Roy, *Jihad and Death: The Global Appeal of Islamic State*, New York: Oxford University Press, 2017.

7 Asef Bayat, 'The Coming of a Post-Islamist Society', *Critical Middle East Studies*, Fall (1996), pp. 43–52. The preliminary ideas and perspective offered in this chapter have been further developed and revised in subsequent publications, notably Asef Bayat,

Post-Islamism: The Changing Faces of Political Islam (Oxford University Press, Oxford, 2013) on which this section of the current chapter draws.

8 See writings, especially by Olivier Roy and Gille Kepel, on the subject.

9 Some of the published works include Husnul Amin, 'Post-Islamist Intellectual Trends in Pakistan: Javad Ahmad Ghamidi and his Discourse on Islam and Democracy', *Islamic Studies*, vol. 51, no. 2 (2012); see also special issue of the *Sociology of Islam* on 'Post-Islamism'. Before it was closed down, the Turkish *Zaman* newspaper published dozens of articles on the idea of 'post-Islamism'. A Google search for the word 'post-Islamism' gives well over two million results.

10 On different types of secularism see José Casanova, *Public Religions in the Modern World* (University of Chicago Press, Chicago, 1994).

11 See Rachid Ghannouchi, 'From Political Islam to Muslim Democracy: The Ennahda Party and the Future of Tunisia', *Foreign Affairs*, September/October (2016).

12 Ibid.

13 See for instance Kerem Oktem and Karabekir Akkoyunlu, 'Exit from Democracy: Illiberal Governance in Turkey and Beyond', *Southeast European and Black Sea Studies*, vol. 16, issue 4 (2016), pp. 469–80.

14 Asef Bayat, 'Green Revolt', in *Life as Politics: How Ordinary People Change the Middle East* (Stanford University Press, Stanford, CA, 2013).

15 The survey was conducted in 2016 in Jordan, Palestine, Tunisia, Algeria and Morocco; see Mark Tessler, Michael Robins, Amany Jamal, 'What the Ordinary Citizens in the Arab World Really Think about the Islamic State', *Washington Post*, July 27, 2016.

16 See Abu-Ibrahim al-Raqqawi, 'Inside the Islamic State "Capital": No End in Sight to Its Grim Rule', The *Guardian*, February 21, 2015. In Raqqa, women cannot work or study outside home, cannot leave home alone, nor take a taxi alone; they are constantly watched in public by the morals police called *hesbah*; see 'Report from the Capital of Daesh: Raqqa Narrated by Women', Radio Zamaneh, 26 Esfand 1394, in Persian.

17 See Humeria Iqtidar, 'Islamism in Pakistan: Islamist Spin-offs and their Contradictory Trajectories', in Bayat, *Post-Islamism*.

8

Relocalizing the National and Horizontalizing the Global

Saskia Sassen

Introduction

One critical feature of the current phase of capitalism is a proliferation of systemic edges inside national territory. I conceptualize such systemic edges as the point where a condition takes on a format so extreme that it cannot be easily captured through the standard measures used by governments and experts. The key dynamic at these edges is expulsion from the diverse systems in play – economic, social, biospheric. Thereby, what lies beyond such an edge becomes conceptually and analytically invisible, ungraspable. Each major domain has its own distinctive systemic edge or edges – thus, the edge is constituted differently for the economy than it is for the biosphere or the social realm. This type of edge is foundationally different from the geographic borders of the interstate system.

The core hypothesis is that we are seeing a proliferation of such systemic edges originating partly in familiar conditions – the decaying Western-style political economy of the 20th century, the escalation of environmental destruction, and the rise of complex forms of knowledge that far too often produce elementary brutalities. The expulsion logics I focus on are just a few of the many that might exist; they are, generally, more extreme than whatever expulsion logics existed, for instance, in the preceding Keynesian period. Further, these expulsion logics are also evident beyond the West, as I argue particularly in a long chapter on environmental destruction in *Expulsions* (Sassen 2014) called 'Dead Land Dead Water'.

The Need to Develop New Instruments for Analysis

In my earlier work (Sassen 2006, 2007) I developed methodological and conceptual elements to cut across the weakened categories developed in the 1950s for studying the interstate system. I identified a variety of vectors that allow one to track processes whatever their geographies. Thus, my intent there was not to contest the weight of interstate borders, but rather to study how a given process scales globally. What are the instruments – of the law, the economy, the social, the cultural – that have been and continue to be developed to enable the making of cross-border processes. One result of that inquiry was that perhaps the critical question marking the contemporary period is not so much the weakening of inter-state borders than who has the power to *make* new types of borderings (Sassen 1991, 2006).

The current work on the systemic edge in *Expulsions* (2014) and on the importance of situating ourselves at the fuzzy edges of a paradigm rather than in the strong center in *Before Method: Analytic Tactics* (2013) represents an additional conceptual instrument. It does not override or contest the earlier (1991, 2006) work. On the contrary, it often builds on that earlier work and takes it further, both theoretically and empirically, by calling for the need to de-theorize – to go back to 'ground level' – so as to see these new alignments. There is a need to de-theorize in order to re-theorize. For instance, I compare a highly polluting industrial complex in Russia and one in the US, and ask what matters more to understand the current period, that one has a long communist trajectory and the other a long capitalist trajectory or that they both have vast capacities to destroy the environment.

Inserting the environmental question here serves to triangulate what is otherwise a mere comparison that uses conventional variables (capital-ism versus communism). It enables a third knowledge space to emerge. Thereby, it helps us go beyond traditional comparisons: we leave behind the Cold War and organize our research and interpretation in terms of what is urgent or meaningful today, with the environmental question representing one such significant current issue. This kind of third dimen-sion takes on specific contents and meanings depending on the domain or variables I focus on. For instance, I explore the growth and privatizing of prisons in the US and the growth and privatizing of refugee camps. Both grow, and both have increasingly private sector interests at work. My question becomes: Are these two very diverse formations, with such different specifics, actually systemic parallels, each adapted to its particular environment? This is a methodological and interpretive practice that recurs continuously in *Expulsions*.

Furthermore, the extreme character of conditions at the edge helps make visible what may also take place via more moderate instances inside the system – a bit less equality in the earnings distribution or the small symptoms of climate change we experience every now and then. In the spaces of the expelled, we find far sharper versions, from middle classes that have lost it all to dead land and dead water. In this regard, I conceive of the systemic edge as signaling the existence of *conceptually* subterranean trends – trends we cannot easily make visible through our current categories of meaning. From there, the importance of positioning my inquiry at the systemic edge, where a condition takes on its extreme form and in that process also escapes our conventional measures and representations.

A key source of these expulsions is a mix of elements often experienced (and admired) as requiring specialized knowledges and complex organizational formats. One example is the sharp rise in the complexity of financial instruments, the product of brilliant creative classes and advanced mathematics, that often winds up destroying healthy non-financial firms. Another is the complexity of the legal and accounting features of the contracts enabling a sovereign government to acquire vast stretches of land in a foreign sovereign nation-state. And yet another is the brilliant engineering and innovations that make possible types of mining that destroy land and water bodies. In my work I explore the extent to which we have reached a point in our advanced political economies where complexity tends to produce elementary brutalities.

What is expelled and the conditions of those expulsions vary greatly. This is one reason why it is not easy to see these diverse expulsions as emerging from shared emergent dynamics. I include a broad range of processes and conditions under the notion of expulsions. What marks them all is their acute character. They range from the impoverishment of the middle classes in rich countries to the eviction of millions of small farmers in poor countries due to the over 300 million hectares of land acquired by foreign investors and governments since 2006. Most familiar are the growing numbers of the abjectly poor who give a whole new meaning to poverty, and the displaced warehoused in formal and informal refugee camps. Then there are the minoritized in rich countries warehoused in prisons and able-bodied unemployed men and women warehoused in ghettoes and slums. Some of these expulsions have existed for a long time, but not at the current scale. Some are new types of expulsions, such as the 14 million households in the US whose homes were foreclosed in a short and brutal history that lasted a mere decade. In short, the character, contents, and sites of these expulsions vary enormously across social strata and across the world.

The globalizing of capital and the sharp rise in technical capabilities have produced scaling effects that break historical records. What may have been minor displacements and losses now become massive expulsions. I found that simply understanding this scaling as more inequality, more poverty, more technical capacity, and so on, is not helpful.

An organizing question running through my work on the notion of 'expulsions' is whether these diverse instances across social strata and urban rural divides, across the Global North and Global South divide, are the surface manifestation or the localized shape of deeper systemic dynamics that articulate much of what now appears as unconnected. These dynamics might be operating at a more conceptually subterranean level than the familiar formations through which we understand our current condition. We rely on markers such as capitalist economy, communist China, sub-Saharan Africa, and so on, to give a familiar shape and meaning to facts and events that might actually be originating in unfamiliar systemics. To that end, I use the notion of subterranean dynamics – strictly speaking, conceptually subterranean – in that they are invisible to us who remain attached to older categories of meaning. New dynamics may well get filtered through familiar thick realities – poverty, inequality, economy, politics – and thereby take on familiar forms when in fact they are signaling accelerations or ruptures that generate new meanings.

A Quick Remapping of the Operational Space of Economic Power

Two profound shifts stand out beginning in the 1980s, and they are happening across the world. But they evolve with highly specific characteristics in each locality. One is the material development of growing areas of the world into extreme zones for key economic operations. On the one hand are the global outsourcing of low-wage manufacturing, services, and clerical work to areas with low wages and weak regulation. At the other extreme is the active worldwide making of global cities as strategic spaces for advanced economic functions; this includes cities built from scratch and the often brutal renovating of old cities. The network of global cities functions as a new geography of centrality that cuts across the old

North–South/East–West divides. And so does the network of processing zones for outsourced labor. One geography concentrates on global wealth and the other on global cheap labor.

The second is the ascendance of finance as a core capability in the contemporary global economy. The network of global cities is a strategic operational space in both the Global North and Global South. Finance in itself is not new – it has been part of our history for millennia. What specifies finance in the current era is the capacity to develop extremely complex instruments and to benefit from electronic networks and their enormous multiplier effects. This rise of finance is consequential for the larger economy. While traditional banking is about selling money the bank has, finance is about selling money it does not have. To do this, finance needs to invade nonfinancial sectors to get the grist for its mill. And no instrument is as good for this as the derivative. The result is an extreme escalating of the value of finance as measured by outstanding derivatives.

Inside capitalism itself we can characterize the relation of advanced to traditional capitalism as one marked by extraction and destruction. At its most extreme this can mean the immiseration and exclusion of growing numbers of people who cease being of value as workers and consumers. But it also means that traditional petty bourgeoisies and traditional national bourgeoisies cease being of value to the larger system. These trends are not anomalous or the result of a crisis; they are part of the current systemic deepening of capitalist relations, and so is the rapidly shrinking economic space in Greece, Spain, the US, and many other developed countries.

From the perspective of this systemic logic, the natural resources of much of Africa and good parts of Latin America and Central Asia count more than the people on those lands count as consumers and as workers. When this happens, we have left behind earlier forms of capitalism that thrived on the accelerated expansion of prosperous working and middle classes. Maximizing consumption by households was a critical dynamic in that period. But its importance keeps diminishing as finance and extraction take over.

Beyond the Rich: Predatory Formations

Besides the concept of the systemic edge and the associated concept of expulsions, another central category I have sought to develop and deploy to capture the particularity of the current period is that of predatory *formations*. I conceptualize these as going well beyond the common notion of the power of the rich. Such formations include pieces of law and accounting, technical capacities, the willingness of the executive branch of government to see with the eye of global corporations, and more. These predatory formations break through the edges of established features of, and notions about, the economy, government, and policy. In other words, the current phase cannot simply be explained in terms of the concentration of income and wealth in a small group at the top. The rich by themselves could not have brought about the massive shifts we have seen over the last 30 years.

Today's vast destructive processes are often complex assemblages of aims and instruments (legal, technical, etc.). The expulsions of people from reasonable lives can be a secondary effect, even if the minoritized are more likely to appear as targeted because they are more vulnerable and marked. I see much of what constitutes expulsion as beyond targeting. Expulsion is even more brutal than targeting: these men and women do not count at all; they are not in the picture. Targeting might set in if they resist before being expelled, but a lot of the destruction is rapid, anonymous or faceless, and total. Indeed, the expelled in this particular period are increasingly diverse: they belong to an enormous diversity of groups, places, projects, and histories. These expulsions touch the discriminated minorities and mainstream middle classes.

One element here is my emphasis on the fact that remarkable new tools at the disposal of powerful individuals and firms actually begin to constitute formations where these users are just one element, rather than masters of the domain, so to speak. The other elements include, among others, advanced mathematics and communications, machines that can literally move mountains, global freedoms of movement and maneuver for top-level executives that allow them to ignore or intimidate national governments and their laws, and increasingly international institutions (global firms, the IMF, etc.) that force compliance with their agenda. And then there are Western governments, central bankers, the IMF, and kindred international institutions, all now pushing the need to reduce excess government debt, excess social welfare programs, excess regulation, which are all geared toward reducing social services and assistance to the disadvantaged.

This is the language of today's key order-making institutions in the West and increasingly elsewhere. One effect and aim is the de facto project of shrinking the space of a country's economy, although not the economic profitability of the corporate sector. It entails the expulsion of growing numbers of sectors and types of workers who are no longer valued. In its simple brutality, the transformation of Greece illustrates this well: the massive and rapid expulsion of small, modest-profit-making firms and of the modest and not-so-modest middle classes from jobs, social and medical services, and increasingly their homes. This sort of process is taking place in many countries, from the familiar case of Spain and Portugal to the less-recognized case of Germany and the Netherlands. Even countries with growing employment, such as the US, have in fact shrunken the space of their economies, as is evident when we include the sharp rise in the numbers of the long-term unemployed, of the incarcerated, and of the small modest firms that are dead.

We must not forget the earlier periods of regions that now seem hopeless, whose better times have been forgotten by many observers as if their hopelessness were an intrinsic constitutive element of their cultures. Beneath today's wars and dismembered societies in much of sub-Saharan Africa lies an earlier period of mass manufacturing, growth of the middle classes, growth of thriving market towns and capital cities, and governments developing infrastructures and health and school systems. Before it broke down, Somalia was a fairly prosperous society, a fairly well-run country even if autocratic, with a well-educated middle class. Or, consider Russia, where today's huge numbers of homeless people, the abandoned elderly and the growing numbers of very poor without access to social services are also a new development. Communist regimes in the Soviet Union and Eastern Europe had welfare states that took care of their citizens.

One effort in *Expulsions* along these lines was to make visible the crossing into the space of the expelled – to capture the visible site or moment of expulsion, before we forget. The villagers and small farmers evicted from their land due to the development of palm plantations soon disappear in the vast slums of megacities where they materialize as slum dwellers – completing the erasure of their past as small farmers with knowledge about plants and crops and weather. Government employees in Greece cut out of their jobs in the name of European Union (EU) demands to cut the debt become part of the mass of unemployed, soon not recognized as erstwhile government employees. Stretches of dead land, poisoned by toxic emissions from factories or mines, are expelled from working land, best forgotten.

New Geographies of Centrality and Marginality

There have long been what I refer to as transversal circuits – that is, circuits that cut across familiar, well-established divisions. In past work, I

decoded some of the circuits originating in the 'West' that have historically cut across diverse histories and geographies through war, trade, slavery, annihilation of indigenous peoples, and more (see *Territory* 2006:
chs 2 and 3). And I have especially studied and conceptualized today's
versions of such transversal circuits.

Among the latter, I have documented empirically the active making of
distinct geographies of power/privilege/extraction that began in the 1980s
and cut across the traditional divides of the modern interstate system (North
and South, East and West). These transversal geographies of privilege and
power can comfortably coexist inside countries with many of the traditional
divides that continue to operate, notably the lack of health care and easy
access to food and water in the Global South, and the ongoing existence of
a strong Communist government structure in some of the East.

I make quite a bit of the fact that these new transversal geographies
can coexist with older divides. The elites of Nigeria are more at home and
more oriented toward the elites of London and Mumbai than they are to
the poor and modest middle classes in their own country. In this sense,
also, these new geographies have the effect of disassembling societies and
cultures, as well as their territories and their national states (see *Territory*
2006: chs 5, 7, and 8; *Expulsions* 2014: chs 1, 2, and 3). Parts of these
territories are built in the image of the richest cities across the world, enabled by the latest technical developments, while other parts are completely
neglected, not even supplied with running water and electricity.

These geographies of centrality incorporate particular sectors (leading
cities, corporate elites, the rich, the executive branch of the state, including its central bank, major public-owned corporations, and more). And
they expel the rest. Thus, a country with vast stretches of impoverished
localities that lack all the basics, from health care to education, may nonetheless put its limited resources in developing its key city so that it can
be a hub in one of these global geographies of centrality. There are many
examples, some familiar, such as Abuja in Nigeria, and some just emerging, such as Luanda in Angola. The so-called rich countries did more or
less the same, beginning in the 1980s, eventually cutting social services
and countrywide infrastructure upgrading, while promoting the glamoriz-
ing of their key cities. I develop this in *Cities in a World Economy* (2018)
and in the two editions of *The Global City* (1991, 2001). I have also found
that the making/justifying of these emergent transversal geographies has
been a powerful tool for mobilizing, persuading, and justifying the larger
cross-border corporate project.

In the past, the British Empire wanted the whole of Africa, Spain wanted the whole of Latin America, and so on. Today's powers want only specific components of the diverse national territories across the world within which they operate. Once done extracting the minerals, or the water, or the crops, they exit and move on to the next set of sites for extraction. These are mobile geographies that leave behind land and sites destroyed by their use, which are in fact expelled from these geographies of centrality – expelled to the zone of dead land and dead water. Another instance is the expelling of much of the traditional middle classes: once a key actor in the making of an industrial- and consumption-based economy, these are now increasingly useless from the perspective of these geographies of centrality. In short, it is not only the 'lumpen', the refugees, and other such desperate people who become 'human waste'. These are, then, increasingly particularized geographies of centrality, ready to expel people, places, and chunks of the biosphere.

Conclusion: Going Back to Ground Level to Cut Across Our Knowledge Silos

As indicated earlier, one of my core arguments to get at the current condition is that we need to go back to 'ground level' as a way of de-theorizing, or destabilizing master categories and powerful explanations, in order to re-theorize. We cannot do without theory if we are to go beyond the empirics of complex configurations and processes. Nor am I arguing that one person by herself can do that re-theorizing. Rather, my image is one of unstable meanings, which generate a need for collectivizing the task of grappling with the issues discussed thus far. We might aggregate these as (a) emergent conditions (e.g., the strengthening of global cities and the neglect of hinterlands); (b) transversalities that exit our master categories (e.g., the fact that prisons and refugee camps may increasingly share features); and (c) dynamics that erase contents (e.g., when environmental destruction is so absolute that the result is not simply degradation, but dead land and dead water).

One effort in my recent work is to find resonances between very different types of expulsions, such as long-term imprisonment and long-term refugee camps. These are never put in the same knowledge space. Each is examined on its own terms, by very different types of experts, and never put in conversation with each other. In contrast, I make a strong point about the need for bringing very diverse conditions in conversation with each other. It generates a mode of researching that insists on de-theorizing in order to detect features that take on very diverse contents and formats in each condition: in the social sciences, prisons and refugee camps are placed in radically different, unconnected, conceptual spaces. For instance, I insist on prioritizing the enormous capacity for environmental destruction of both Russia's Norilsk nickel-producing complex, the largest in the world, and the vast gold mining operations in Montana, regardless of the fact that one belongs to a communist history and the other to a capitalist one.

In short, and to illustrate what is a very broad set of domains, I argue, for example, that today's capacity to destroy air, water, and land overrides the master categories of the interstate system. Further, the spaces of the expelled are not like the 'regular' spaces where most of social, political, and economic life keeps taking place. But neither are they simply non-spaces. Indeed, the spaces of the expelled in this particular period arise from increasingly diverse groups, places, projects, and histories.

I explore whether there is a disjuncture between the surface individuality of distinct types of expulsions and deeper dynamics that underlie them all. It is this possibility that leads me to the notion of expulsions. This is one feature they all share, even when the character and the contents can vary enormously. The fact of multiple specialized fields of research, knowledge, and interpretation, each with its cannons and boundary protecting methods and theories, does not help in this task.

At its most brutal my hypothesis is that beneath the specifics of each instance lie emergent systemic trends shaped by a few very basic dynamics, no matter their enormously diverse visual and social orders. In that sense, empirical research and conceptual recoding must happen together: empirically, it may look 'African' or 'Italian', but are these markers of an earlier era still helpful in understanding the character of our epoch. To invoke a somewhat self-evident case, China may still have much that is communist, but its growing inequality and most recently impoverishment of the more modest middle classes might be rooted in deeper trends it shares with a country as diverse as the United States. They are very different countries, and will remain so for a long time. Nonetheless, they may both 'host' finance, speculation-driven tendencies, and a push for maximizing profits. And these parallels and their consequences on people, places, and economies may well turn out to be the more significant change of our times. Clearly, this focus on the interiority of countries contrasts with the far more common focus on national borders as the sites where change is happening.

References

Sassen, Saskia (1991) *The Global City: New York, London, Tokyo*. Princeton, NJ: Princeton University Press.

Sassen, Saskia (2001) *The Global City: New York, London, Tokyo*, 2nd edn. Princeton, NJ: Princeton University Press.

Sassen, Saskia (2006) *Territory Authority Rights*. Princeton, NJ: Princeton University Press.

Sassen, Saskia (2007) *A Sociology of Globalization*. New York: W.W. Norton.

Sassen, Saskia (2013) 'Before method: Analytic tactics', *Pluralist* 8(3): 79–82.

Sassen, Saskia (2014) *Expulsions: Brutality and Complexity in the Global Economy*. Cambridge, MA: Harvard University Press/Belknap Books.

Sassen, Saskia (2018) *Cities in a World Economy*, 5th edn. Thousand Oaks, CA: Sage.

9

Social Movements: The Core of General Sociology

Michel Wieviorka

The choice of such an issue – 'The Futures We Want: Global Sociology and the Struggles for a Better World' – is not banal. Yes, we social scientists have to think globally, and yes, a main task for sociology is to analyze struggles. But this is not obvious. And let me add immediately that struggles for a better world should be opposed to hatred and violence, destruction and self-destruction, to social anti-movements, but that they deserve also not to be researched too independently: it is very useful to study together the Good and Evil, struggles for a better world, on the one hand, and on the other hand, racism, xenophobia, antisemitism, terrorism, etc. They share or could share articulated concepts.

If we want to discuss concepts, theory, or empirical knowledge, we must be able to do it in good intellectual conditions. Social scientists have a strong interest for cultural diversity, and many among them have discussed multiculturalism or cultural rights; they know that speaking and writing in one's own language is important. Their international associations, such as the International Sociological Association (ISA), used to have two or three official languages (English, French and Spanish for ISA): let me hope that among the struggles for a better world, social scientists will fight for multi-lingualism in their own practice.

An intellectual turn, or shift, appears clearly in these texts. Until recently, there was a deep feeling that uncertainty and difficulties make the world in which we live more and more dangerous, difficult, and that the idea of progress, or at least of social progress was no longer acceptable. What appears here is, on the contrary, the idea that a better world is possible. That there is a future, that the idea of progress is not totally obsolete. And that we are at a moment when we have to face a real civilizational change or at least that we need it. This return to the futures is not a regression.

And if we can imagine a better world, and consider that there is a future, it is first of all due to the action of collective actors. Social movements, struggles, protests – whatever the categories we use – bring the possibility of a better world. And not or at least not only technocrats, elites, economic or political leaders.

Usually, the category of 'social movements' is just one among many other fields or issues in sociology. Deciding that this specific meaning of collective action is at the very center of general sociology means that we admit that it offers a key perspective, including for those that study other sociological issues, such as institutions, organizations, development, delinquency and crime, norms, etc.: movements are here the core of social life and its transformations. This means also a strong criticism of analyses that have interest only in the center, or those that are top-down. Yes, social scientists bring useful knowledge when showing in their work interest in the 'horizontal', the 'neighborhoods', in those actors that introduce logics from below – bottom-up. In the 'pueblos in movement', in feminism, decolonization, indigenous perspectives for instance. Having social movements at the very center of sociological analysis is not obvious, and deserves discussion. It is a challenge, and I appreciate the way this challenge is dealt with here.

It is true that this category 'social movement' belongs to sociological tradition, but also to non-scientific vocabulary, and that within the social sciences, there are different possibilities of conceptualization. Should we still call 'social movements' these new forms of collective protest, or at least some of them such as revolutions in the Arab or Muslim world, the Indignados in Spain, or Occupy Wall Street in the United States, like in the 1960s and 1970s, when two main sociological schools liked to discuss and oppose two concepts, the one proposed by Alain Touraine, the other one by Tilly? Maybe not, since these recent struggles are also cultural, civic, ethic, and since the social itself is not necessarily the main point – even if it is important not to forget this main issue that we can call 'inequalities'. This could mean that we must invent a new concept, invent new tools, new analytical categories, maybe new methods in order to analyze correctly new forms of action.

If we consider struggles as important, if for instance we research on social or global movements, we must be aware that is maybe dangerous, or difficult – we should all remember Giulio Regeni, a young sociologist who was working on trade-unions in Egypt and was murdered in Cairo, and we should always support our colleagues that have to deal with an authoritarian regime, such as in Turkey today.

Empirical work, fieldwork, is necessary; theory too, this is clear. And this also means that we should never stop being highly critical, including when we consider the so-called 'open society' and its tendencies to become in fact closed, with those movements that I call anti-movements, nationalism, in search of satisfactions only for their nationals. Dealing with theory includes from my point of view introducing some reflections on the necessity of new or renewed concepts and methods, with a key point: we need a stronger capacity to articulate concepts, and not to be only specialized in some 'silo'. This leads quickly to the idea of pluri-disciplinarity, and not only with academics belonging to one discipline. This leads to the project of producing knowledge not only on actors, but with actors – as we shall see, migrants, imprisoned people for instance could be considered from this point of view.

Among other academic disciplines, we should take very seriously into account the necessity to deal with history when trying to project ourselves in the future. This is not an easy challenge. Let us consider, for instance, the recent 'revolutions' in the Arab and Muslim world, that began in Tunisia in December 2010. From a sociological point of view, they included dimensions that made them belong to the family of social movements; they were acting in name of such values as dignity or democracy. From a historical perspective, they ended, with the exception of Tunisia, in terrible violence – the authoritarian regime in Egypt, the civil war and Islamic State in Syria, the chaos in Libya, etc. The historical synthesis cannot be the same as the sociological analyzes, even if sociologists are able to analyze the passing from a struggle for a better world, to violence, hatred, terror, and war. To say it differently: combining sociology and history, sociological analysis and historical synthesis is necessary, but is not such an easy task. But it is not possible to have a strong interest for the future without having a too strong interest for the past.

Social, cultural, democratizing forms of action are not directly political, are not dealing with the level of the state, and here there is a great challenge, a political one for the actors, an intellectual for us: how do these actors pass from the social, the cultural, the civic, to the political? And what can be the framework of this articulation, when one knows that the meaning of even very local struggles is so often global, while the political system has been built at the national level?

10

Epilogue

Alain Touraine

Editor's Note: The following text is based on the author's concluding remarks at the Closing Plenary of the Third ISA Forum.

On Asef Bayat

Asef Bayat asks the question: can we imagine a Muslim democracy? I immediately answer in a negative way: a Muslim democracy is as impossible as a Christian, Jewish or Buddhist democracy. God's law is by nature eternal; men's laws are by nature historical: what a majority has decided another one can cancel.

The basic condition for democracy is laicity, which is the separation of political power from religious authority. In Western Europe the German Emperor, later on the French King and a couple of centuries after, the King of England, have freed their national political power from the universal authority of the Pope.

But when civil society, that is, economic power and more precisely a ruling class, have imposed their interests on entire countries, democracy can become impossible and has been constantly threatened. It has survived only because it has received a new universal legitimacy from the quasi-religious and philosophical idea of human rights, first in England and Holland, then in the United States and France, as far as the Western World is concerned.

The concept of human rights, including its concrete legal consequences, is not social because it is universal while there is no universal nation or society. There is no democracy without the recognition of universalistic principles of political legitimacy. Both new Islamist leaders and neo-orientalist Western thinkers must abandon the idea that Orientals are by nature pre- and anti-modern. It is the downfall of 19th-century Western 'progressive ideologies' which has provoked the present day Islamophobic movement. And incidentally, I would mention at least one example of a Muslim democratic movement: in southern – that is Iraqi – Kurdistan the motto of the recent winners of free elections was: 'Independence, Laicity, Feminism'.

On Akosua Adomako Ampofo

As far as this general problem is concerned, Africa, according to Akosua Adomako Ampofo from the University of Ghana, seems to be more advanced than Islamic Middle East Asia because many African thinkers and leaders today seem to combine in many elaborate ways a real respect for universalistic modern concepts with the deep wish to 'return to an African future'. Reading her text feels like reading the Humboldt brothers in Berlin in 1807 after the battle of Jena, or Petöfi or Kossuth in Hungary.

National, cultural and political consciousness has constantly been linked with the universalistic orientations of the Enlightenment. The unrealistic opposition of these two cultural and political trends was quite understandable during the period of national liberation movements but has actually been overcome in many parts of the world, in Africa as much as in Latin America. A careful study of all types of combination of these two opposed and complementary cultural and political trends should be a major field of study for sociologists of all parts of the world.

On Todd Gitlin

But the recombination of supposedly opposed orientations is not enough to propose a correct analysis of our futures. Todd Gitlin is profoundly right to add two more dimensions to this problematic. First of all, a very concrete social dimension of our so-called development is the exploitation of human labour by owners of mines, mills and ships.

The fact that this factor has received an unjustified monopoly in some post-Marxist analysis cannot justify unacceptable under-evaluations of social conflicts and especially of class conflicts in the analysis of our past and of our future.

The second dimension is the irrational exploitation of natural, environmental and human resources, which was as dramatic in 17th-century

Scotland as it is everywhere today. So that our main preoccupation should be to combine these four main dimensions of social analysis rather than trying to demonstrate 'the surdetermination', to speak in Althusserian language, of three of these dimensions by the fourth one. As Todd Gitlin rightly says, as a general conclusion of his chapter, 'We need more encompassing theory' and he adds for sociologists that such an enlarged theory must help us to move to a sustainable world.

On Markus S. Schulz

But our last word must be directed to ourselves, sociologists. And a clear answer comes, as we rightly expected it, from the main architect of this forum, Markus S. Schulz. His answer is convincing because it is surprising.

All four dimensions of a general analysis of the future refer to mass phenomena and long-term trends. So that when we come to the question 'what are the most important and efficient answers mankind gives to this major problem?' we expect to read a long list of international initiatives or, in a more modest way, of intellectual and professional debates.

And many of us may be surprised that Markus Schulz devotes a large part of his attention to Chiapas's Zapatistas and more precisely to Subcomandante (that means not Maya-born) Marcos (Schulz, 1998, 2007, 2016). I cannot conceal my satisfaction, as a personal participant in the 'Intergalactic Convention' that met in La Realidad, Chiapas, in 1996 and as a member of a research center that has devoted much time and many publications to these indigenous Mexican social movements (Le Bot 1997, 2009), because, along with other international observers, including the Portuguese Nobel Prize recipient Saramago, I can testify to the consciousness of these poor peasants who live near the Guatemalan border of offering answers to worldwide problems, in the same way as the first trade union members – British, Belgian and German miners or steel mill workers – were conscious of the importance of the future of the International Association of Workers they belonged to. Yes, I believe that in our world, which seems to be dominated by a globalized financial system and by militarized regimes, small and often defeated social movements can bring some very important elements to theories and practices that can transform our future. I think Markus Schulz is right.

This opinion, which is probably not an isolated one, is based at least partly on the fact that functional, fitting, well-adjusted behavior often tends to increase in our societies, just as there are inequalities, dominations and self-destruction, while critical or even marginal behavior is necessary to enable our society to correct its mistakes and crimes and to increase its creativity, at least when criticism and protest are not rapidly transformed into authoritarian conformity with new rules and privileges.

Our present day globalized world is so extremely one-sided and so completely dominated by smaller and smaller political or economic oligarchies that we should recognize that social grassroots movements, even when weak or twisted, are often more efficient and necessary for our survival than many technological innovations or politically manipulated revolutionary ideologies.

Let's remember that field work is a major instrument of sociological research, especially when we try to discover and understand the most active defenses of human fundamental rights. Do you not think that the most advanced type of field work is to discover and reinforce the process of formation of human actors as creative and free subjects whose fundamental rights and dignity must be recognized and even institutionalized?

References

Le Bot, Yvon (1997) *Le rêve zapatiste*. Paris: Seuil.

Le Bot, Yvon (2009) *La grande révolte indienne*. Paris: Éditions Robert Laffont.

Schulz, M.S. (1998) 'Collective Action Across Borders: Opportunity Structure, Network Capacity, and Communicative Praxis in the Age of Advanced Globalization', *Sociological Perspectives 41*(3): 587–616.

Schulz, M.S. (2007) 'The Role of the Internet in Transnational Mobilization: A Case Study of the Zapatista Movement, 1994–2005', *World Society Studies* (I): 129–156.

Schulz, M.S. (2016) 'Debating Futures: Global Trends, Alternative Visions, and Public Discourse', *International Sociology 31*(1): 3–20.

Index